Being an Academic

The role of academics in universities worldwide has undergone unprecedented change over the past decade. In this book, Joëlle Fanghanel discusses the effect on academics of modes of governance that have fostered the application of market principles to higher education and promoted flexibility and choice as levers for competition across the sector. She explores what it means to be an academic in the twenty-first century with reference to six 'moments of practice' through which she analyses the main facets of academic work and the responses of academics to this neoliberal drive. *Being an Academic* effectively examines the frameworks that govern academic work and academic lives, and the personal beliefs and ideals that academics bring with them as educators and researchers in higher education. It argues that there is a rich, critical, empowering potential within the academy that can be harnessed to counter the neoliberal stance and shape a meaningful contribution to modes of enquiry that deal with complexity and uncertainty in a global world.

Drawing on empirical research collected from a global range of academics, this book examines how academics respond to structural challenges. It offers a re-appraisal of the main dynamics underpinning the professional and intellectual engagement of academics in today's universities to feed a reflection on possible responses to the complex contemporary world with which the academic endeavour is engaged. The themes explored include academics' positioning towards:

performativity and managerialism
regulation and professionalization of practice
the relation to learning and students
the discipline
research
globalization.

Each chapter includes vignettes illustrating the theme addressed, a discussion with reference to the context of policy and practice, published literature and illustrative reference to empirical data collected through interviews amongst academics in the UK, Europe, North America, South Africa and Australia.

Providing a fresh look at the role of academics in a changing world, this book is essential reading for all those engaging in higher education research, lecturers new to higher education, and practising academics navigating through their complex role.

Joëlle Fanghanel is Director of the Institute for Teaching, Innovation and Learning at the University of West London, UK.

Being an Academic

Joëlle Fanghanel

Routledge
Taylor & Francis Group

LONDON AND NEW YORK

First published 2012
by Routledge
2 Park Square, Milton Park, Abingdon, Oxon OX14 4RN

Simultaneously published in the USA and Canada
by Routledge
711 Third Avenue, New York, NY 10017

Routledge is an imprint of the Taylor & Francis Group, an informa business
© 2012 J. Fanghanel

British Library Cataloguing in Publication Data
A catalogue record for this book is available from the British Library

Library of Congress Cataloging in Publication Data
Fanghanel, Joëlle.
Being an academic : the realities of practice in a changing world / Joelle Fanghanel. — 1st ed.
p. cm.
LB2331.F34 2011
378.1'25—dc22
2011011490

ISBN: 978–0–415–57370–2 (hbk)
ISBN: 978–0–415–57371–9 (pbk)
ISBN: 978–0–203–81823–7 (ebk)

Typeset in Galliard and Gill Sans
by Prepress Projects Ltd, Perth, UK

Pour Nadj, Ozzi et Sof

Contents

Acknowledgements   viii

Introduction: turbulent moments of practice   1

1   The managed academic   15

2   Learning to teach in higher education   31

3   Conceptions of students and learning   48

4   The discipline   66

5   Being a researcher in higher education   82

6   Academic globalism and worldly becoming   97

Conclusion   114

References   120
Index   136

Acknowledgements

I owe many thanks to the fifty colleagues in universities in the UK and elsewhere who agreed to be interviewed for my research over the years and to whom I promised anonymity. Without their generous and inspiring contribution, this book could not have been written. I want to thank especially Ronald Barnett, Glynis Cousin, Anna Jones and Bruce Macfarlane, who read the manuscript of this book with dedication and generosity. Their insightful comments guided my reflection in the final stages of writing, and I wish to express to them my gratitude for the sharpness and diligence of their critique. I wish to thank too Roger Brown, Sue Clegg, Vaneeta D'Andrea and Lisa Lucas, who kindly offered comments on specific chapters as work was in progress. I am indebted too to the many colleagues and friends who generously shared their views with me through discussions as I was writing this book. I wish to thank especially Murray Saunders, whose discussions with me sowed the seeds of this book, and Ian Scott, who was the first to encourage me to write this book during a visit to Cape Town. My thanks go too to Philip Mudd at Routledge for his unfaltering support and guidance throughout this project. Finally, I wish to acknowledge the colleagues at the University of West London who supported me in this endeavour and Peter John especially for the interest he took in the making of this book. Any errors or omissions in this text are of course entirely mine.

The data informing this book include thirty-three interviews that are connected to studies which are already in the public domain (Fanghanel, 2004, 2007a, 2009a,b,c; Fanghanel and Trowler, 2008). Another seventeen interviews were undertaken specifically for the present book. Chapter 6 also uses data that were collected for a separate study (Fanghanel and Cousin, 2012).

Introduction

Turbulent moments of practice

Openings

This book explores what being an academic means today. It focuses on academics' experience of the realities of practice. To capture this experience, it takes account of the frameworks that govern academic work and lives, and of the personal beliefs and ideals academics bring with them as educators and researchers in higher education. In the process, it disentangles espoused conceptions of the academic, as they might emerge from academic folklore or depictions reflecting policy incentives or management regimes, from lived experience. It is not seeking to be an encyclopaedic review of academic work and practices, or a practical guide. It offers rather a re-appraisal of the main dynamics underpinning the professional and intellectual engagement of academics in today's universities to feed a reflection on possible responses to the complex contemporary world with which the academic endeavour is necessarily engaged. This book focuses on the teaching and learning, and research aspects of the academic role. As a result of this emphasis, important aspects of the transformations taking place in the academy are left aside, such as, for example, the examination of cadres in management, or of administrative staff who support student learning. The space I study is that of academics in their relation to students, research and teaching, with reference to their discipline and their work communities. Although the lived experiences and environments I explore extend beyond the UK context, this book is inevitably grounded in that perspective.

Roles can be examined as reified descriptions of practice (the specification of what is expected of academics, couched in normative terms), or as instantiations of academic identity – the way academics appropriate and inhabit those prescribed roles. It is the latter on which this book concentrates, and issues related to conditions of employment and rules of engagement are not examined. The focus is deliberately on the main aspects of the academic role with a view to delving into its inherent complexity. I call those different aspects of the academic role 'moments of practice' to convey a sense of elasticity and fluidity, and to locate each within a constellation of other moments. I examine six moments of practice – the managed academic, the early career academic, the relation to students and learning, the academic as discipline specialist, the academic as researcher, and the academic in a global context.

Stating that the academic role is complex and multi-faceted amounts to a platitude; analysing this complexity, and probing the nature of its facets, is, however, a worthwhile enterprise. In the sociological view of practice adopted in this book, academic roles are not seen as scripted; they are constructed and inhabited through navigating the tensions between structures, the communities in which practice takes place, and academics' own positions towards structures. Complexity and diversity stem as much from the structural conditions in which academics work (institutions, policy frameworks, academic conventions) as they do from the specific ways in which they respond as individuals to those conditions (their agentic positioning towards those, and their own beliefs about education and the academic endeavour).

The object of this study (being an academic) is not just complex, elusive and multi-faceted; it is located at the heart of a web of tensions – some structural, and some related to the beliefs and values that academics hold about education, which are examined later in this introduction as educational ideologies. Practically, the necessity for academics to handle increasingly diverse and specified tasks and roles (Whitchurch, 2008a; Malcolm and Zukas, 2009; Macfarlane, 2011) demands of them a complex and composite set of skills, knowledge and competences. They operate in a space that needs to accommodate the demands of market-oriented practices, and yet contain the aspirations academics have for themselves and for their students, and their passion for knowledge – what Rowland (2008: 353) has called 'intellectual love'. They also iterate between the requirements to teach generic knowledge that is transferable to the world of work, and their commitment to a discipline. The aptitude to work ubiquitously to ambiguous scripts – across teams and space and beyond specialisms – is, I suggest, inherent in the demands made on academics in today's higher education. Before I proceed to examining the context from which this book has emerged, and the framework from within which it is constructed, a word of caution is extended in respect of the terminology used throughout this book. I refer to 'the academy', 'universities' or 'academics' as though they were entities easily amenable to conceptual capture; using such essentializing terminology masks the complexity, nuances and differences within the field. It is simply a pragmatic shortcut to name plural referents.

Universities today

Universities are places like no other workplaces; and academic work is akin to that of few other professions. The university, as an institution, functions through the contribution of subject specialists working within – and across – disciplines, engaged in complex relations with the student body.

Their work processes are neither entirely tangible nor susceptible of yielding entirely predictable outcomes. Universities are also positioned in turbulent spaces. *Organizationally*, different levels of practice come into play to generate teaching, learning and research, with tensions and fluxes between them. *Ideologically*, universities have complex hybrid – increasingly contested – missions; in particular, tensions between the desire to educate and the necessity to provide entry into employment pervade the work and discourse of the academy. *Politically*, they provide a fertile ground for economic battles and competitive incentives.

Quite apart from this unique status of universities in the social field, rapid changes over the past three decades or so have had a significant impact on the way academics work within them. These changes reflect the social, political, economic and technological trends that have affected most of the Organisation for Economic Co-operation and Development (OECD) countries and impact too on emerging economies. Broadly, these can be attributed to the following key factors, which are closely related:

- the *decline of the welfare state* signalled by gradual state disengagement from public sector control and increased private contribution (Salter and Tapper, 1994; Deem *et al.*, 2007; Tapper, 2007);
- the imposition of *market mechanisms* and *managerial control* broadly referred to as 'neoliberal managerialism' (Deem *et al.*, 2007);
- the view that higher education serves *economic imperatives* – what Musselin has called 'industrialization of academic activities' (2007: 182), Ozga 'the economizing of education' (2000: 24) and Lyotard a 'professionalist function' (1984: 49) for universities;
- long-standing and now worldwide pressures to democratize *access* to higher education (Trow, 1973), and a concurrent increasing stratification of the sector;
- the impact of *globalization* on higher education practices, policies and markets (Robins and Webster, 2002; King, 2004; Lingard and Ozga, 2007); the related issues of ubiquity of practice, blurring of working boundaries and 'increased access to workers' (Gappa *et al.*, 2007: 32) through *technology*;
- easy *replicability* of goods and texts; and rapid *obsolescence* of a knowledge base that is constantly expanding and recombining at high speed;
- questionings in terms of the university's status as a transmitter, preserver and creator of *knowledge* (Gibbons *et al.*, 1994; Readings, 1996; Robins and Webster, 2002; Barnett and Di Napoli, 2008) and the impact on academic identities, on the research agenda and on visions (or lack of) of educating for a complex world (Luke, 2007).

Although at whatever point in time one examines the workings of universities, it seems to have been characterized by constant evolution (Musselin,

2007) and some nostalgia for a golden age, today's practices and expectations in the academy hardly compare with what they were only two decades ago. This is true of academia, of the field of education generally and of many other social fields. However, because of the mythology surrounding the academy – which includes the 'ivory tower' tale (Robins and Webster, 2002), the solipsistic bastions represented by its constituent disciplines (Becher, 1989), the quaintness of its doings and whereabouts (Goffman, 1959; Bailey, 1977), its unabated claim for and reclaim of autonomy (Dearlove, 1997; Harland, 2009) and the questions around its purpose and function as a social field – the work and ways of academics remain relatively mysterious outside the academic 'tribe' (Becher, 1989) itself. In a rather economical understatement, one of the academics I spoke to expressed this in the following way:

> Academic labour in society in general isn't understood that well. People don't really know. A lot of people don't really know what you do and a lot of times, students don't either – and maybe we are not very good at enlightening students about what academic labour is about.

There is much diversity within the higher education field; diversity across countries, and within. There is diversity also within institutions. I show in this book that, when examined from the perspective of the responses of academics to their environment, the differences that emerge do not always coincide with the strong structural chiasmic categorizations often used to distinguish universities worldwide – research-intensive, sandstone, Ivy League, teaching-oriented, public, state institutions and so on.

The academic profession

An enduring vision of the academic is that of a pursuer and transmitter of knowledge; this image of the teacher–scholar–researcher is anchored in the German Humboldtian tradition of scholarship in which research and teaching go hand in hand. In reality, research was introduced as a significant driver of the activities of western universities only after the Second World War (Brown, 2010). There are still a few countries where research is located within specialist institutions outside the university sector. Equally, the doctorate became the preferred qualification for entry into the academic profession only well into the second half of the twentieth century. Although the majority of universities today are access-based rather than research-intensive institutions, this view of the academic persists. In reality, career patterns and translation of academic roles into practice are essentially diverse, even if individual academics still hold a sense of the ideal academic position (Evans, 2009).

Some twenty years ago, Ernest Boyer (1990) outlined as a typical academic trajectory the kind of linear coherent steps that take an academic from an early focus on research to increased emphasis on teaching and service commitments in the latter stages of her career. This ideal type does not represent what is happening in practice. In a recent international study involving over twenty countries, Locke and Bennion (2010a: 4) drew attention to the 'considerable variation' between different groups of academics. The increased emphasis on linking higher education with industry and the world of work has played a significant role in changing the make-up of the academy. Today's curricula (oriented towards the world of work) have led universities to accommodate an increasing number of professionals from other fields – lawyers, engineers, media specialists, artists – or other areas of the public sector. Amongst those, a number of academic workers have what has been described as 'portfolio careers'. As self-employed specialists, they contract their expertise in flexible ways, in various contexts (Fenwick, 2003). As a result of more complex understandings of teaching and learning, and of student support, the boundaries across different categories of staff in universities have also become blurred (Gordon and Whitchurch, 2007; Whitchurch, 2008a,b; Macfarlane, 2011).

Economic imperatives also play a significant role in shaping the academy. Universities, although not strictly public sector institutions, like many areas of the public sector, have been affected by regular cuts in funding, state disengagement and private sector competition (King, 2004; Slaughter and Rhoades, 2004; Welch, 2005; Tapper, 2007; Brown, 2010). Resulting rationalization of provision and increased casualization of academic staff have significantly affected the evolution of academic work and of working patterns, leading to what has been seen as a 'proletarianizing' of academics (Readings, 1996). Reliance on adjunct faculty or fixed-term contracts (Dearlove, 1997; Rhoades, 1998; Finkelstein, 2007; Gappa et al., 2007) is widespread. Resource shortages (Finkelstein, 2007; Meek, 2007; Santiago and Carvalho, 2008) and severe cases of low staff qualifications (Galaz-Fontes et al., 2007) have also been reported in some areas of the sector.

Technology has of course profoundly changed the way academics teach and research, and the speed at which they are expected to work. This, coupled with expectations of increased devotion to work, encapsulated in the idea of the 'ideal worker', has engendered more mobile work patterns and tangible gender inequalities (Gappa et al., 2007). Technology enables speed and transparency of processes that impact significantly on practices and the expectations of students and managers. Last but not least, increasingly sophisticated understandings of learning, and of the impact on learning of the educational environment, have also played a part in making the academic role more complex.

In this context, many studies on the academic profession have spoken of a 'crisis of the professoriate' (Musselin, 2007: 175). Musselin has suggested that the changes affecting the academic profession must, however, be considered within the broader changes affecting all professions, the pace of which has significantly accelerated over the past decade or so. In this sense, she suggests that we are witnessing an attenuation of the differences between the academy and other professional sectors. I will show in this book that the agency of individuals – the way they act in practice in response to the constraints of their environment – is resisting this attenuation as academics bring to their roles their own beliefs about education, and their own values.

Academic identities

My study bears on academics in action. It focuses on academic identities at work and their interaction with the environment of practice. Identities are instantiated in positions that academics adopt in their practice, with reference to their own subjectivities (emotions, beliefs and understandings), histories and capabilities. Although I do not systematically deconstruct these in my analysis, identity components that contribute to their positioning are many. They include the intersection between academic and other aspects of identity – for example class, race and gender (Clegg, 2008). This richness is woven through my analysis, which conceives of identities as constructed, relatively fluid and influenced by academics' biographies and habitus, their positions within the academic field and their own ideological beliefs about education. Academics' positions in practice also reflect their beliefs about the discipline, teaching and educational goals, and towards other aspects of their environment – research, technology and the world more broadly. Other aspects of their role, including the relation to other disciplines, and to the management and administration functions of universities, also play a part of that positioning.

Clearly, identities are read at the micro level of practice, in which the focus is on individuals. However, they are inscribed within the wider world (society at large) and within existing practices and policies at the level of the institution, and communities and groups of co-workers in departments or units. The focus of my analysis is on the congruence of academics' positioning with, or, on the contrary, dislocation from, the agendas that frame their practice. I examine the positions that academics adopt towards and within the moments of practice under study in a way that is reminiscent of Robert K. Merton's (1968) framework of adaptation to a norm. Merton established a typology that has often been used or adapted to examine how individuals position themselves towards a given agenda (e.g. Trowler, 1998; Henkel, 2000). He identified four types of positioning towards a norm. Broadly, people who tend to comply can be associated with categories of 'conformity' (accepting an agenda because they believe in it) or 'ritualism' (a form of surface compliance); and those who reject it offer resistance through 'innovation' (adapting it to their own ends) or 'retreatism' (rebellion and refusal). Although Merton's typology is quite useful as a heuristic, I have incorporated it into the broader stance towards agency in this book – that is, by examining individuals' degree and form of agency (e.g. their acceptance, rejection or subversion of any given agenda).

Educational ideologies and academic values

To illustrate the *value* tensions inherent in academics' positionings, I turn to educational ideologies. Educational ideologies are normative models of education. In the sociological perspective I am working from, they provide a strong theoretical framework for accounting for beliefs and values that can be held about the role of universities and of academics as educators, with reference to their beliefs about social order, distribution of and access to resources, and knowledge, for example. They can be examined at two levels; nomothetic (prescriptive) models of education at the macro level of policy and governance (e.g. a vocational curriculum) translate into ideographic (situated, unique) ideological positionings in the practice of academics (how the academic will approach this vocational stance in practice). Educational ideologies permeate all moments of practice examined in this book.

There are different ways of presenting ideologies of education (see, for example, Trowler, 1998; Saunders and Machell, 2000; Robeyn, 2006; Young, 2008) but the central issues are the same – the relation of education to work and the economy, and to human and social development. An initial distinction, however, focuses on the contrast between education perceived as an end in itself and education as a means to an end. In the first perspective, learning is valued for its own sake, as a goal in itself. It is a view of education based on Humboldt's sense of the unity of knowledge (and of the strong connection between teaching and research), or on Cardinal Newman's notion of the university as a 'seat of universal learning' (Newman, 1852, Discourse 5). In the second ideological perspective, education is perceived with reference to its economic value. A 'human capital' theory (Schultz, 1963; Becker, 1993) of education promotes a view of higher education as the lever of economic capacity, and/or as a point of entry into the labour market. I suggest that the latter is a dominant model in higher education.

Other dimensions have however been identified outside those two main orientations. These include privileging personal growth and social progress (Trowler, 1998) or education as a human right (Robeyn, 2006). A related reflection on the challenges presented by emerging economies has promoted education as 'capability development' based on Amartya Sen's development economics work (Sen, 1985, 1999, 2002). It focuses on the development of emotional, intellectual and personal capabilities to promote equity, equality (with an emphasis on addressing gender inequalities), social justice and enhancement of social contexts, with the aim of empowering individuals in the life choices they make (Nussbaum, 2000; Walker, 2006; Nixon, 2011).

In this book I will use a simplified framework to talk of ideologies. I have identified *production* ideologies, which refer to the human capital theory described above, with a focus on the direct link between higher education and the world of work (Saunders and Machell, 2000); *reproduction* ideologies, which convey conceptions of the virtue of education for its own sake, and an emphasis on 'heritage' (Trowler, 1998: 67) and transmitting the tenets of a discipline – and advancement of knowledge in the field – to reproduce the next generation of discipline experts; and *transformation* ideologies, which emphasize education for social, personal, human or global transformation. These ideologies represent *intentions* on the part of educators. So, although both production and reproduction ideologies can trigger transformation in the student, the intention of the educator in each paradigm is focused on the relation to the world of work and to the discipline respectively.

Production educational ideologies are concerned with developing aptitudes and skills relevant to the real world of work; education is valued as economic investment. The forms of knowledge privileged in this paradigm are practical, work-related knowledge and meta-cognitive skills (learning how to learn, becoming an effective and successful learner). The keyword in this paradigm is 'context-dependent' knowledge – which Michael Young (2009: 15) has defined as follows: 'Context-dependent knowledge tells individuals how to do specific things. It does not explain or generalise; it deals with particulars'.

Briefly, Young contrasts this with 'context-independent' knowledge, which he defines as 'theoretical knowledge' (p. 15) and refers to as 'powerful knowledge'. At the risk of oversimplifying, Young's social realist position on knowledge posits a critique of education that privileges context-dependent knowledge and advocates the need to take students 'beyond their experience' (Young, 2008: 23) through access to context-independent (theoretical, propositional) knowledge. The educational enterprise then becomes one of 'endeavouring to ensure that learners have access to the rules of [knowledge] production in its different forms' (p. 63). A production ideology by contrast plays down the intellectual and social dimension of higher education. It values utility and immediate relevance.

Reproduction ideologies have also been labelled as 'liberal' (with reference to liberal arts all-rounder views of education), 'traditional' (Trowler, 1998) and 'neo-conservative traditionalism' (Young, 2008). In this paradigm, learning has intrinsic value, students are driven by curiosity, they learn for the sake of getting to know and with a view to finding their own place and their own voice within the discipline they have embraced. In this perspective, the university is seen as a site for transmitting and advancing knowledge, and validating it through peer-review critique, often with a view to shaping the next generation of educators and knowledge producers. Knowledge is perceived as separate from the knower – residing in a set of corpora and/or legitimized through objectively reached consensus. So broadly, a reproduction ideology is contiguous to the humanist views of education dominant in the nineteenth century, in which knowledge was seen as a means of advancing individuals and society through reproducing and advancing society's existing order. Reproduction is also about privileging official (peer-reviewed) knowledge, and there is some contiguity with Young's notion of context-independent or 'powerful' knowledge mentioned earlier – although Young stresses the 'hidden agenda' (reproduction of existing social patterns) that prevails over episte-mological concerns in what he calls 'neo-conservatism' (Young, 2008: 20). This conception works from within a framework that emphasizes discipline expertise, abstract and codified knowledge, and the primacy of intellectual achievement.

In transformation ideologies, including those reflected in activist models of education such as the capability development type mentioned earlier, the emphasis is on the transformation of individuals or of society (e.g. Apple, 1993, 1995; Freire, 1996; Barnett, 1997). These models often include a strong emphasis on the moral axiological dimension of education. They apprehend education as an emancipatory tool and focus on social justice, equity, criticality and self-development. Transformation ideologies problema-tize both reproduction and production views of education. They contain a social critique of educational frameworks that generate self-exclusion and the reproduction of inequalities (Bourdieu and Passeron, 1977; Apple, 1995; Bernstein, 1997, 2000; Reay et al., 2001; Yosso, 2005). Although they may privilege experiential and constructed knowledge, there is no strong claim to this; post-constructivist (context-independent) views of knowledge are not incompatible with this ideological position.

As indicated earlier, educational ideologies operate at the level of academ-ics' own beliefs about education (and how this is evidenced in their intentions and actions), and at the structural level of policy, policy texts and the aspira-tions of universities as translated into local policies, teaching and learning strategies, or mission statements, for example. However, in the field of *lived* practice, there is a considerable degree of fuzziness, fluidity and overlap in the way individuals position themselves towards those ideologies. I will show throughout this book the complex and overlapping positioning of academics in the moments of practice I examine.

Apart from the values inherent in those ideologies, institutional autonomy and academic freedom are also perceived as fundamental values in higher edu-cation (Bleiklie, 1998: 299). Based on the German concepts of *Lernfreiheit* (the freedom to choose what, how, when and where to learn) and *Lehrfreiheit* (as an entitlement to teach and disseminate to those both inside and outside of the university), of which US scholars were early adopters (Gappa *et al.*, 2007), academic and institutional freedom hold a prominent place in aca-demic discourse, and in the academic psyche. Historically, in a number of higher education systems – those of the UK, Australia and North European countries, for example – there has been a relative intellectual independence from the state moderated by more or less financial dependency. In other countries, such as Germany, for example, universities and federal government (Länder) work very closely together. In France (Musselin, 2009) or Italy (Boffo and Moscati, 1998) universities historically have had little autonomy, being closely dependent on the state for funding and appointments. In the US where dependency is mostly on private donors and large foundations, universities have been relying more on peer review and collegial responsibility (Rice, 2006) to regulate their practices. With a view to generating a reflection on the notion of academic freedom, and with reference to the complex conceptions and enactments of academic practice I uncover in this book, I turn to Latour's (2009) suggestion – that 'heteronomy' might be a better term than 'autonomy' to describe the status of the academy today. Without endorsing the rather political way in which he has developed this notion, I use this term simply as an acknowledgement of the degree of local and global interdependencies the academy finds itself enmeshed within.

Structure and agency

This book focuses on academics' responses to the context of practice in which they operate as educators in order to capture complexity and nuance. Theoretically it locates individuals (at the micro level of practice) within the broader collective and historical contexts of wider society, and of the communities of practice that impact on their practice. It conceptualizes the social world as a material and historicist object made of a web of complex processes and flows, subject to interactions and overlaps. My focus is on the interaction of individuals with this social world – here more specifically the context of higher education. Epistemologically, this study adopts a post-constructivist standpoint by taking the view that knowledge of the world is mediated through collective socially produced knowledge based on a constantly re-appraised consensus on enquiry that contributes to elaborating a body of valid and legitimate knowledge which provides the learner/researcher with abstract verified propositions that transcend the immediate context. This position is distinct from naïve positivist notions of realism that do not problematize the complexity of apprehending or representing reality, and from notions that reduce the world to an individual's empirical perception of it.

The question of agency is central to any work investigating (higher education) practice, as it provides access to agents' *purposeful* action (as resulting from reflection, choice and positioning) towards the social structures that frame their everyday practice. The way that agents and structures interrelate is central to the problematics of social theory (see, for example, Bourdieu and Passeron, 1977; Giddens, 1984; Archer, 2000; Sawyer, 2002), and crucial to understanding practices from non-naïve realist perspectives. It is the analysis of that relation that helps us understand the impact of structures on practice, and account, for example, for individuals' positioning (within a group or towards a specific agenda), and for phenomena such as policy reconstruction (Ball, 1994; Saunders and Warburton, 1997). Positioning towards any policy, curriculum frame or management agenda is complex and rarely unidirectional (Thomas and Davies, 2005; Fanghanel, 2007a; Smith, 2008; Clegg and Smith, 2010). It is intricately linked with the ways that individuals are continually engaged in constructing and re-constructing their sense of self in the world to maintain 'a precarious sense of coherence and distinctiveness' (Alvesson and Willmott, 2002: 626).

In earlier work, alongside the reflection of Ashwin (2009), for example, I pointed to the limitations of social practice theory, in its various forms (Giddens, 1984; Engeström *et al.*, 1999; Lave and Wenger, 1999; Wenger *et al.*, 2002), in adequately accounting for the relation between structure and agency (Fanghanel, 2009a), some frameworks overemphasizing intersubjectivity and the scope for agentic positioning in practice (e.g. Lave and Wenger, 1999), others overemphasizing systems and losing agency within them (e.g. Engeström *et al.*, 1999). Bourdieu's is an example of a framework that loses agency. He sees fields as highly structured, historically coherent and logical entities in which agents have little choice or autonomy – their trajectories determined by their position in the field and the habitus they bring to it. The relation of agents to structures is at the heart of the conundrum, with a tendency towards what Archer (2000: 7) has called 'upwards conflation' (in which the individual is oversocialized and with no real agency) or 'downwards conflation' (which reduces society to the individual and denies historical and social structures). These issues were not fully resolved through adopting Giddens' position on structures. As Archer has judiciously noted, although Giddens' structuration theory appears to solve the issues of upwards conflation and downwards conflation, it brings in what she calls the problem of 'central conflation' whereby structure is acknowledged only in its immediate dialectic relation to action/agency, anchoring the question in the present, and losing any sense of a historicist dimension or social continuity in that relation (Archer, 1995). Social practice theory also confines agency to an analysis through the concept of 'knowledgeability' (Giddens, 1984), which does not account for the materiality (including gender) or affective components of agency, and denies any account of the intractability of structure in some areas of practice (Fanghanel, 2009a).

Without wanting to dwell too much on these theoretical issues, I am presenting in this book a view of agency that draws on Archer's notion that agency encompasses the natural, the practical and the social domains of reality (Archer, 2000), and is therefore multi-dimensional. I perceive of the relation between agents and structures as being at the same time historicist (and therefore ideological and theoretical), material (not only a set of properties), embodied (and therefore relating to real bodies in real spaces), emergent (from specific contexts) and fluid (not grounded in static views of identity). Agency can be collective (as in activism, e.g. Clegg, 2006) or individual (shaping selfhood and at the same time a manifestation of the self). Examples of analyses carried out within groups of academics (Trowler, 2008) illustrate well the collective dimension of agency, but I am focusing mainly in this book on examining individual responses to the context of practice.

Respondents and data

The data were collected over a period of years through interviews connected to studies that are already in the public domain (Fanghanel, 2004, 2007a, 2009a,b,c; Fanghanel and Trowler, 2008) amounting to thirty-three interviews; another seventeen interviews were undertaken specifically for the present book. In total, fifty interviews were carried out amongst academics representing twenty institutions and five different countries. Chapter 6 also uses data that were collected for a separate study (Fanghanel and Cousin, 2012). The data are cited anonymously, with reference to discipline, country of practice or type of institution only when this is deemed of importance. This is mainly because of the broad range of posts held by respondents – which do not always coincide across different countries, or even across institutions – and also to avoid stereotyping responses with reference to a country, or type of institution. This book represents contributions from a variety of institutions but I have no desire to reproduce literally the logic of stratification that nefariously pervades the academy; the emphasis is on individual responses, accepting that the locus of practice can be – but as suggested earlier is not always – constraining.

The theoretical framework outlined above does not diminish the scope for interpretative analysis of the data, but interpretations of meanings are not made in isolation from the respondent, or from the researcher's own awareness of the context, structures and historicity from within which respondents speak. I shared with my respondents through my own rooting into higher education a degree of implicit knowledge about practice. This 'practical consciousness' enables the researcher to go beyond the 'discursive consciousness' of respondents (Giddens, 1984: 7) – that which it is possible to say and which is often rendered through coherent and reasoned accounts of activity. I often refer to these interviews as 'conversations', as they were conducted in a dialogic manner (Knight and Saunders, 1999), and were intended to be communicative and beneficial to both the interviewer and the respondents.

Finally, in terms of the status of the data presented in this book, the fictional vignettes (with the exception of vignette four, which includes a short extract from a policy publication and adapts to the genre of the vignette the words of one of my respondents) are a compound of situations I have witnessed or experienced and do not necessarily emanate from the interviews, whereas in-text respondents' quotations are drawn from the interview data and cited *verbatim*. The vignettes are not representative of my sample; their purpose is rather to illustrate the points I am making in any specific chapter.

Summary of chapters

This book examines six moments of practice that capture the main aspects of the academic role. In exploring the lived experiences of academics within those roles, it highlights the complexity of academics' positionings towards the management of practice intended in the set of regulations that frame their work.

Chapter 1 focuses on the responses of academics to the policies in place in universities to manage practice and performance, broadly labelled managerialism. In a context in which higher education is subjected to neoliberal modes of governance that foster competition and market principles within the sector, and seek to engender flexibility and choice as levers for competitivity, these policies promote competition, flexibility, and management and display of performance. This chapter shows how this agenda can compete with academics' own understandings of the processes and finalities of a university education. It explores ways in which *managed* academics adopt, adapt or resist the imperatives of this framing of practice.

In Chapter 2, the focus is on early career academics, and the *learning to teach* moment of practice. The requirement for early career academics, in an increasing number of countries around the world, to undertake systematic training to develop knowledge and expertise in teaching, learning and assessment has generated a range of initiatives that have promoted relatively glossy (unproblematized) ways of thinking about teaching. This chapter outlines specifically the limitations of this enterprise through an analysis of the reality gap between theory and practice. It identifies transfer of knowledge, structural and ideological dissonances.

Chapter 3 explores the relation of academics to the student body through a focus on *conceptions of student and learning*. It examines contrasting types of discourse about students and learning and academics' own conceptions of students with reference to their educational ideologies. Although the student as 'consumer' is identified as the dominant model, other conceptions are explored that emanate from academics, and provide sophisticated responses to the consumer model. It is suggested that those could serve as a basis for re-imagining the relation between students and academics.

Chapter 4 focuses on the *discipline* moment of practice. It considers academics' complex constructions of their discipline and the relation of these conceptions to the beliefs and understandings of the wider world that academics bring with them in the academic space. It suggests that disciplines, at the moment of their enactment in practice, are more than abstract epistemological constructs, or structural entities. Discipline conceptions are significantly influenced by the external world and the way academics relate to it.

Chapter 5 discusses the *research* moment of practice and argues that universities are increasingly accommodating diverse modes of research. This multimodality is explored through an incursion into the make-up of the research space, and an exploration of the choices available to academics in what I call managed (broadly funded, peer-reviewed) research. This chapter suggests that alternative modes of research, in particular scholarship on higher education practice, can provide inspiring models for the academy.

Chapter 6 examines academic *globalism*. It probes what being global means in practice for academics. It considers the tensions between economic, intellectual, ethical and ideological stakes in the global question. It reports specifically on the way that academics experience globalism in practice and discusses what I have called 'worldly becoming' as an exploration of the strategies through which the academy can harness the potential brought about by globalization to engage in shaping understandings of how to live with uncertainty and 'supercomplexity' (Barnett, 2000).

The conclusion chapter draws out the most salient points concerning these six moments of practice – which broadly will have examined the academy's various forms of responses to the neoliberal agenda underpinning academic practices in today's universities. In this final chapter, I suggest that these responses provide a rich, critical and empowering potential that can be harnessed to develop approaches to educating students and practising research that address the complexities of today's world.

Chapter 1

The managed academic

Introduction

The first moment of practice examined in this book is that of the managed academic. In this chapter I consider the responses of academics to the mechanisms gradually put in place over the past three decades or so to control and regulate academic performance. I discuss the impact of this form of management, and the positioning of academics towards it. In doing this, I begin to draw the outlines of the matrix on which I am reading academic practices and identities in this book. Subsequent chapters will further explore the positioning of academics towards the frameworks discussed in this chapter.

The term 'managed academic' is used to capture the impact of the forms of management put in place in universities over the past three decades or so to manage performance and practices, and often described as managerialism. Briefly, managerialism describes the application of private sector management approaches to the public sector. It has been defined specifically as:

> a general ideology or belief system that regards managing and management as being functionally and technically indispensable to the achievement of economic progress, technological development, and social order within any modern political economy.
>
> (Deem *et al.*, 2007: 6)

Practically, specific instantiations of managerialism (see Deem *et al.*, 2007 for subtle distinctions between corporatist, neoliberal and technocratic managerialism) have generated cultures and practices in the academy that are underpinned by market-like principles, based on metrics, control and display of performance. The term 'managed academic' has been used by Richard Winter (2009) to signify an identity schism between those academics whose values are congruent with the discourse of managerialism (academic manager) and those whose values are incongruent with it (managed academic). With an emphasis on the academic profession in the United States, Rhoades

(1998: 4) has also spoken of faculty as 'managed professionals'. His focus was on unionized faculty, and the restructuring of the academic profession in the late 1990s in the United States. Mine encapsulates both the ideological and the rationalizing intentions inherent in the forms of management prevailing worldwide in higher education today. I do not discuss specifically the extent to which the academic endeavour is a profession on a par with that of dentists, doctors or lawyers, for example – which Rhoades takes for granted; nor do I seek to emphasize dichotomies between managed and managers, as does Winter. My focus is rather on the degree of agency within what has become an increasingly regulated and controlled form of engagement.

The model of management in operation in today's universities has emerged from the neoliberal modes of governance that have been deployed in the public sector since the 1980s (known in the UK as the 'rolling back' of the state). These reforms have triggered a re-appraisal of the relation between the state, public organizations and the nation, signalling in particular the beginning of a questioning of the welfare state (Deem *et al.*, 2007; Tapper, 2007; Brown, 2010; Nixon, 2011). In universities, these management practices have emerged against the backdrop of the massification drift in the 1960s and of the social and political crisis of the 1970s. In practice, in universities, managerialism translates into systems and processes – greatly enabled by instantaneous computing of information and data – that monitor, evaluate and display academic performance. This has resulted in academics getting a strong sense of being managed, and some witnessing a 'deprofessionalization of academic work' (Trow, 2002: 311). In this chapter I examine first the structural background – how these regimes have emerged within higher education institutions more or less the world over. I then turn to the responses of academics in practice, showing that the positions adopted are complex, and less of one piece than one might imagine. Although some have found their place within the academy by fully harnessing this agenda, others have resisted it vehemently. On close inspection, a picture appears that is more nuanced and complex than this simple alternative suggests.

The governance of higher education

Over the past three decades or so, in the West at least, the state has sought to establish competitive markets in all areas of social practice (health and education, for example) that had previously been under its control and protection. This so-called neoliberal approach fosters competition and market principles, and seeks to engender flexibility and choice as levers for competitivity. In higher education, the mode of governance through which this is delivered includes a combination of control and disengagement. This has put universities in positions in which they are at the same time more subjected to regulation and financially less supported – or supported in more focused ways. 'Remote steering' (Neave, 1998: 266) governance has encouraged self-monitoring by universities in order to promote efficiency from within, so to speak, through processes of self-analysis, self-surveillance and proactive disclosure. The somewhat paradoxical combination of state disengagement and increased regulation has been facilitated through an underlying compact that outlines the main aspects of the nation-state–universities problematics in a neoliberal perspective:

- the introduction of *market mechanisms* and *market theory* into higher education, in which higher education institutions compete for funds, student places and reputation;
- the gradual move from principles of *accountability* to principles of *self-regulation* of the university sector to sustain the market orientation (i.e. being competitive through externally recognized measures of quality);
- alongside this market inflection, and more broadly under the impact of neoliberal ideology, which emphasizes the link between industry and higher education, an erosion in practice of the *notion of education as 'public good'* (Bleiklie, 1998; Deem *et al.*, 2007; Brown, 2010; Nixon, 2011);
- the related gradual – and significant in some countries – shift of the financial burden onto the individual student;
- hybrid funding models (Naidoo and Jamieson, 2005; Marginson, 2007; Tapper, 2007; Brown, 2010), which have further inflected diversification and competition;
- fragmentation in the stakeholders' landscape (Scott, 1995; Musselin, 2009), with an increasing number of interest groups and the introduction of 'quasi-state' organizations (Tapper, 2007);
- principles of regulation that have shifted from a focus on *input* (number of students, estate capacity, etc.) to a focus on *outputs* (measurements of quality and targets such as completion rates, student success and satisfaction, etc.) resulting in a retreat from concerns about fair distribution of resources and redress of inequalities (Marginson, 2007; Musselin, 2009);
- the increasingly ubiquitous view of higher education as having an economy-related mission.

Although those neoliberal trends are identifiable to a lesser or greater extent in most parts of the world, it would be incorrect to read this inflection towards marketization, financial state disengagement and increased regulation as all of one piece. There are important local variations in terms of the manner in which system changes were introduced (Musselin, 2009), the pace of change, the degree of state distantiation and the reference to supra-national frameworks – particularly in Europe with the Bologna Process (Huisman, 2009). Transition to the 'evaluative state' (Neave, 1998) has been mediated in more or less subtle ways by different governments. It required legislation in some countries – in mainland Europe, for example (Musselin,

2009) – but was based on consultation with stakeholders elsewhere – in the UK, for example (Tapper, 2007). Bleiklie has noted that, although the rise of the evaluative state appears to 'signal profound changes in the way public authorities understand academic activity' (Bleiklie, 1998: 310), there is sufficient ambiguity, inconsistency and complexity in the system to guard against predicting management futures in universities. Tapper (2007) and Musselin (2009) reach the same conclusions. Deem and colleagues (2007: 27) propose that 'retreat' from the present level of engagement with managerialist practices is unlikely to be possible. Some, however, predict that neoliberal forms of governance will vanish from higher education as surreptitiously as they pervaded it (Davies et al., 2006). Although clearly the academic profession has been affected by these structural changes in ways that have profoundly changed its workings, this chapter, and more generally this book, will show the nuances and complexities of academics' responses in practice.

Managerialism and performativity

These new modes of governance in the public sector have had significant repercussions on ways of managing performance. 'Managerialism', 'new managerialism' and 'new public management' as loosely related terms designate the forms of public sector management underpinned by the market principles I have outlined earlier. At the risk of oversimplifying one can say that these forms of management have strongly emphasized local devolvement of responsibility, self-evaluation and self-management of performance throughout the public sector. In higher education, these principles have generated new ways of conceptualizing academic work, academic performance, the relationship between the different constituent parts of the university and the relation to society and industry.

Lyotard coined the term 'performativity' in the late 1970s to describe the management 'technology' needed to sustain this ideology. Performativity is an approach that provides 'the best possible input/output equation' (Lyotard, 1984: 46). At the macro level, in respect of higher education, performativity is about securing the best possible contribution of higher education to the best possible performance of the socio-economic system. At the level of universities, this translates into setting up structures and mechanisms that steer, measure and monitor efficiency to generate the best possible performance. For governments, this has meant subjecting performance to public scrutiny through a combination of competitive incentives and the setting up of mechanisms to expose (make visible) and streamline practices so that 'the ability to produce proof' (Lyotard, 1984: 46) is facilitated.

The management of quality in universities is perhaps one of the most significant examples of the performativity principles discussed here, because it affects all academics (and students) and potentially pervades all aspects of academic practice. It is a worldwide agenda (Brennan and Shah, 2000), and, although approaches differ slightly, the trend in state-funded (or partially funded) higher education is towards increased local devolvement of the responsibility for evidencing fitness of provision through quality assurance (QA) processes. In the UK, Australia and Northern Europe in particular, this agenda has been promoted alongside a quality enhancement (QE) agenda. There is a clear theoretical distinction between the two – QA focuses on quality processes, and the achievement of specific objectives, whereas QE seeks to generate a culture of constant re-appraisal and improvement. In practice, the distinction between them is often less stark.

The UK was one of the first countries to establish a system of audits to control and assess teaching quality in universities, with the creation of the Quality Assurance Agency in 1997 (Brown, 2004). This model has been emulated in many countries. Although in the UK there has also been a slight move from a system of inspections to one of enhancement through self-evaluation and peer review (a case in point in the UK being the Scottish model, with a strong focus on enhancement through self-assessment and formative feedback from reviewers), there is no evidence that a softer route will be taken in subsequent iterations. In much of Europe, QA mechanisms have evolved within the framework of the Bologna Agreements mainly with a view to generating homogeneity and comparability of provision across Europe (Ravinet, 2008). Ozga and her European colleagues have suggested that QA instruments have entirely restructured the idea of education in western society and have become a form of 'governance' of themselves (Ozga et al., 2011). In the United States, notwithstanding attempts from the Higher Education Commission (HEC), and a recent experimental attempt by the Mid-West Association at developing some kind of quality framework (the Academic Quality Improvement Programme), the concept of regulation does not exist in the same way. D'Andrea and Gosling (2005) have shown that the approach to quality management is far less bureaucratic, being based on a formative approach avoiding sanction. Canada's enhancement model is close to the US model although based on a more diffuse funding model (Donald, 2006).

Quality assurance models have emerged worldwide. In the Gulf States, for example, as governments recognized the need to develop higher education as a prestige competitive niche, existing QA models have been imported and adapted (D'Andrea, 2009), which includes using the Australian framework (Carroll et al., 2009); accrediting private institutions (Al-Atiqi and Alharbi, 2009); and developing national frameworks with the help and chaperonage of European universities (Kaghed and Kezaye, 2009) and international organizations (Darandari et al., 2009). Other countries where there was no or hardly any (or restricted as in the case of South Africa, for example) post-secondary provision before the 1970s have also started to focus on quality assurance, albeit with much more limited resources than in Europe or the Gulf States, and with a focus on addressing the lack of preparedness of students (e.g. Scott, 2003). China is also heavily influenced by western practices (Jayaram and Altbach, 2006). In the extensive Russian Federation post-secondary landscape, with around 1,000 higher education institutions, priority is given to those institutions that can claim some world-class reputation, the rest being difficult to manage, having expanded beyond the control of the state (Tomusk, 2003). To align itself with the rest of Europe, the Russian Federation has opted for the Bologna model (Tomusk, 2006). Recognizant of the deep crisis in their higher education systems post communism, most Central and Eastern Europe countries have done so too, embracing Bologna with their eyes almost shut, and some hope to reform their own national systems (Kwiek, 2006).

Talking from a European perspective, Ball (2003: 215) has argued that performativity has not only affected 'what educators, scholars and researchers do' but also their identity – 'who they are'. The relation to academic identity and academic agency of managerialism and performativity cultures is central to the issues discussed in this chapter. With a keen eye on the significant body of literature that has established the importance of examining the interface between policy and practice, and the way actors interpret and enact policy (e.g. Lipsky, 1980; Ball, 1994; Saunders and Warburton, 1997; Trowler, 1998; Fanghanel, 2007a; Musselin, 2009; Clegg and Smith, 2010), I show in this chapter, and throughout this book, the manifestations of agency, and the evident tensions that emerge at the micro level of practice where academics are not always responding to the shaping that is sought by the policy maker.

Academic practices and identities in performativity cultures

> The higher education model feels like a superman or superwoman model . . . that you are expected to be able to do anything at any point.

I have often cited these words from one of my respondents, who found academia a stressful and inhumane environment, and one conflicting with her beliefs and values. She was one of a number of academics I have met in the course of my work who felt under considerable levels of stress. Those encounters have signalled to me the importance of academics' own beliefs, understandings and desires about their practice; the impact on those of their disciplines; and the pressures exerted on them as they work to complex and often contradictory agendas. Managerialist approaches have been shown to have significantly affected academic practices and cultures (Trowler, 1998; Taylor, 1999; Henkel, 2000; Prichard, 2000; Deem, 2003). Deem and her colleagues (2007: 27) have suggested that managerialism is 'routinely resisted, avoided and adapted in all sorts of ways', and that those who have 'embraced' it are mainly 'a small minority of academics in management and leadership positions' (p. 27).

The nuances are, in fact, many. Some of the academics I have spoken to brought with them what could be called narratives of despair – stating their frustration at not being able to do their jobs properly and their despondency in the face of what they perceived as anti-learning bureaucracy. Some also conceded to being under stress, sometimes leading to depression and sickness. Others – not necessarily managers – were able to buck the trend, operating relatively freely, seizing opportunities, finding niches for their skills and interests, and enhancing their careers, and their own motivation, through the incentives and prospects available to them – appropriating (and shaping) this agenda to serve their own beliefs and aspirations, eschewing, thus, the sense of being managed. However, I return for a moment to tales of despair through a first vignette that tells of Mary's incapacity to deal with the turbulence.

Vignette one: Mary's encounter with the performativity agenda

Mary is a geography lecturer at a university that states as its mission the delivery of excellent teaching and excellent research. Departments set annual targets for publications. Criteria have been established to select research-active academics – those who will be competing towards the national assessment of research quality. Teaching time with students is measured and recorded. Performance is monitored, reviewed and assessed each year by line managers. The university has recently introduced an appraisal system that covers all aspects of research, teaching and learning, administration and external service, and which includes specific indicators to assess the performance of academics in all these domains. One of the university's strategic objectives is to become more competitive by increasing its rating in international research rankings, and improving its position in the National Student Survey.

This intensive agenda has taken its toll on Mary, who is a very conscientious and dedicated academic. Suffering from stress and exhaustion, she was off on sickness leave for a whole term in the spring. She thinks that she is not the only one who feels the pressure resulting from overwork and constant surveillance, and is convinced that the level of activity in the department is sustainable only because people are just completely exhausted. The highly intensive teaching model adopted at her university is extremely time-consuming because many students come in without the level of academic skills needed to succeed easily – at least, that is how she sees it. With first-year students, she spends a large number of hours just getting students to the point where they can write essays and express themselves clearly. This, says Mary, takes hours and hours, and everyone in the department is completely overworked. She can't think of a colleague who doesn't do work at the weekend. She worries that she may not be

able to achieve the required number of peer-reviewed publications expected
of her. She has noticed that the relationships in the department have started to
get much more segmented – some senior members who wanted to focus more
on the research were passing on their marking to the most junior members
of staff. She likes her department very much, she likes the teaching, she loves
her research, but she thinks that much of the pressure has to do with the
incredible amount of structures and the bureaucratic proliferation of systems
and mechanisms. She feels that academics have come to be imagined as people
who operate like puppets, and she is very worried about the future.

Work intensification

Conceding to unusually heavy workloads is by no means solely the predicament of young academics. Some senior academics I interviewed mentioned
unreasonable expectations from (the often elusive) management (below, the
head of an engineering department):

> The amount of time we have to spend on research is absolutely . . . We
> audit our time. We put in our timesheets. Everyone is doing a huge
> number of hours – I don't think the university would really want to
> accept that anyone is actually doing that number of hours – and most of
> the time, people are doing their research outside the hours they are here,
> as we have a huge teaching commitment.

A senior academic in a research-intensive university was also personally
affected by the demands made on him by his job:

> I have just come away from a period of illness, so I have been away from
> it for a while, but before that it was . . . it was a bit . . . . If there was one
> reason why you wanted to leave, it was that, to take early retirement or
> whatever. Like this grant application I have just put in, the only reason
> I could do it is that I was off sick. Had I been at work, I would never
> have been able to do that. Every day, most of the day would be trouble-
> shooting on this or that, and you can't do it, you can't focus on anything.

Workload pressures inducing high levels of stress, and a sense of being
underrated, were leitmotivs amongst the academics I have interviewed. One
of the latest UK surveys published on stress amongst faculty and staff showed
that 59 per cent of them worked outside normal hours, with 21 per cent
claiming to regularly work more than 55 hours a week (Kinman *et al.*, 2006).
International studies have shown that women – often having to combine
family responsibilities with their professional careers – were particularly
affected by harsh working conditions and restricted access to senior ranks

(Luke, 2000: 291). In order to cope with stress, and redress work–life balance, some of them 'pulled out of the race' (Luke, 2000: 289). At a basic level, beside the specific obstacles encountered by women, academic work is indeed difficult to account for (Fanghanel and Trowler, 2008). The counting of teaching hours – a method commonly used in teaching-oriented institutions in the UK – seems an inadequate and archaic way of accounting for ubiquitous working practices. The significant amount of time dedicated to preparation, service or student support outside of the classroom goes somewhat unnoticed; research is not included in this formula. More importantly, perhaps, it conveys a sense that academic work might compare with work in industry and services, and therefore be amenable to reductionist calculations, as was the case for this respondent:

> It is five hundred and fifty hours annually. So three hours of that five hundred and fifty would be one lecture . . . So you are getting a work profile and that states exactly what you are doing in the year, and how many hours you have been allocated. . . . In reality when you write a lecture for the first time, you spend three weeks and not three hours doing it. So when you look at somebody's worksheet, it is not realistic.

Visualization and transparency

Work intensification as described here results from the significant amount of administration needed to display performance:

> So everything has to be fully documented now. Twenty years ago, we were much more flexible. It is not something I enjoy but I appreciate that it has to be done. Yes you bite the bullet, and you fill in the forms, and you make your lectures available for auditing, you make sure all your syllabuses are up to date, etc. . . . yes there is a little bit more administration involved alongside the teaching, but I accept those, it has to be done.

Despite the weary tone, this academic indicated that this was also 'fairer to students'. The issue of the democratizing effect of performativity cultures was raised several times about different aspects of practice. The positive democratizing effect of managerialist approaches has been acknowledged in the literature (e.g. Deem *et al.*, 2007). Perceived benefits have included *inter alia* 'greater accountability' and 'less irresponsible behaviours' on the part of academics (Davies *et al.*, 2006: 314). There is a thin line, however, between that and the unreflective form of compliance that such practices can induce, as hinted by one respondent:

> I don't believe that this system – with its checks and balances – setting exams, second examiner checks, etc. . . . is actually very helpful. It is basically . . . they are there to cover your back and it can actually produce a

certain amount of 'well, somebody else will look after it'. So it makes you possibly work much harder, but less responsibly.

This academic also commented on the absurd practices that bureaucratic rules could engender. He had been criticized by one of his senior colleagues for informing students of their mid-term test results. A university rule existed – which he had contravened – whereby students were not allowed to know their mid-term assignment grade, which could be disclosed only after students had sat the final examination. 'Nothing is common sense, you know', concluded this academic. Whether absurdities stem from inadequacies in the systems in place, or from inadequate or overcompliant understanding of those systems, is irrelevant in a sense.

To what extent is this visualization (measuring and displaying of performance) informative? Performativity is exercised through instruments and metrics that do exactly what Lyotard said – they assess, compare and display performance. Instruments such as student evaluations, student surveys, examination results, number of PhD students, outcomes of quality audits, research income, citation rates, research papers outputs, all generate data that inform internal and external rankings. The performance of individuals, teams and institutions is thus under constant (semi-)public scrutiny. Comparisons are made at a surface level between elements that may not in fact allow for fair comparisons. Measures such as the Shanghai Jiao Tong, the Times Higher Education World University Rankings or other comparisons that do not make specific allowance for context only carry surface validity. However, universities have become dependent on them to measure and display their degree of competitiveness; willy-nilly, they play the ranking game.

The ironic role of visualization, its declared democratizing value and its limited validity as much of what is being recorded is in fact not actual practice but computed accounts of practice – or 'fabrications' (Ball, 2003: 224) – is worth pausing on for a moment. Brown (2010) has shown how inadequate – and counterproductive as a trigger to choice – was the reliance on information display to inform the market. What is actually happening in practice is partially erased from these public computations. More insidiously, however, it can affect the way that academics and students come to understand learning, and subsequently their mutual relationship as learners and teachers:

> Everything has to be immediately transparent . . . I am not arguing for obscurity for its own sake or anything like that, I just mean some things are hard and you can't necessarily get there cumulatively.

Many of the academics I spoke to lamented the fact that only that which was measurable and visible seemed to matter to the university, and increasingly to their students. Students were believed to be 'strategic'. Several of my respondents stated that students were instrumentalist and wished to focus only on tasks that would earn them credits. They saw students as being as ambushed in the performativity trap as they themselves were. I will discuss this further in Chapter 3, in which I examine the relation of academics to students and learning, and the way that the economic ideology underpinning performativity has affected conceptions of students in the academy.

Streamlining of practice

In order to measure and report in ways that are comparable, streamlining (or attempts at streamlining) has been introduced in many aspects of academic practice – the curriculum; the way feedback is given to students; the experience of students in seminar rooms and lecture theatres; the way virtual learning environments are used; the way students and lecturers interact online; the way academics write research applications. The list goes on.

One of the most significant changes in approaches to teaching in higher education over the past twenty years, the world over, has been the introduction of an outcomes-based curriculum. As a perfect example of rationality and homogeneity, this promotes 'alignment' between what students are expected to learn on a programme of study, what is being taught and what is being assessed, and how grades are allocated (Biggs, 2007). This reform has made the curriculum a highly technical, logical and coherent object. In theory, the democratizing effect of an outcomes-based curriculum is evident. It introduces transparency in the relationship between students and teachers, with clear expectations as to what is going to be learnt. Academics have, in a sense, to 'come out', by clearly stating what will be learnt, how, and how learning will be validated through relevant assessment tasks. In practice, it is much more complicated.

There are many environmental conditions that challenge alignment. A curriculum is always more open than any set of learning outcomes might suggest – there are unintended outcomes; learning occurs beyond those outcomes; evidencing learning through achievement of outcomes does not always denote learning. Students also come to a topic from different perspectives; for them to engage as creative and critical individuals, a degree of flexibility must be maintained. This brings in much unpredictability. Increasingly, too, a curriculum is distributed beyond university boundaries (as in work-based or service learning curricula, for example) where learning outcomes are more difficult to prescribe, and less easy to assess. Moreover, a curriculum is situated within a specific teaching and disciplinary environment, where academics have their own sets of beliefs and values about teaching and learning in their discipline that inflect what and how they teach. The supposedly predictive nature of learning outcomes has, however, affected the nature of the relationship between teachers and learners. One academic I spoke to thought this was deflecting from real teaching, and he vehemently resented this:

I hate the current climate which treats the relationship between the teacher and the student body as a kind of contract such that you're supposed to know exactly in advance what you are going to be doing – here it all is – and they can sort of bring a lawsuit if you don't do justice to that phrase that came up at the bottom of page 3. This is garbage, absolute garbage . . . . That's wrong! This is not the way to go. What if there is something that is more interesting? Or even someone asks a question and you think, 'that's terribly interesting, let's spend next week talking about that', and that wasn't in the plan at all. I should worry. What is more important?

Other academics, however, particularly (but not only) if they were new entrants to the profession, emphasized the other side of the coin and quite favoured the ideology underpinning outcomes-based curricula as exemplifying the professionalizing of teaching and learning, 'dealing students a fair deal', or 'ensur[ing] a level playing field'. Here, the spectre of compliance appears again, as rules are seen as a way of guiding and protecting academics – reinforcing the notion that the neoliberal agenda renders academics risk-averse or 'docile neoliberal subject[s]' (Davies *et al.*, 2006: 307):

We have guidelines about teaching. It is nice to have a little bit to go by, you wouldn't like to go completely blindly with the freedom to teach however you wish because there would be too much variability . . . It needs that kind of framework.

Excellence and innovation

Ball has noted that the technologies deployed to regulate and control performance can open up 'new possibilities for action' (Ball, 2003: 218). He has attached to this optimistic statement a significant health warning, which is discussed later – the risk to the integrity of an academic's identity. Two paradigms have dominated higher education in the past decade to shore up – and give a human face to – performativity. They are excellence and innovation. The vignette below shows how academics can harness the performativity agenda to unleash the new possibilities of which Ball talks.

Vignette two: Theo's focus on innovative approaches to teaching and learning

Theo teaches business management in a large business school and has a keen interest in innovative teaching methods. He has established an array of initiatives within the school to engage large numbers of students in active learning. These involve students working in groups with or without the use of technologies, and generating their own self-help groups to support each other's learning. He initiated a 'web2.0 boardroom' where student avatars worked over a semester in a virtual environment endorsing specific roles and completing real-life and real-time tasks. He also imagined and organized an induction programme for first-year students – lasting a full week – that involved fact-finding and problem-solving activities in various shops and businesses in town, communicating through tweets and IMS. He considers it essential that students should become familiar with interactive technologies and develop sophisticated business skills in the course of their studies. He likes to base his innovations on the experience of others, and belongs to a number of groups and networks that are concerned with the use of technology in teaching business management. One of his most recent initiatives (somewhat controversial according to his colleagues) included real business partners in the design, delivery and evaluation of an international business programme. He secured the contribution of businesses in China, India and Brazil to present real work scenarios to students who designed real solutions that were offered to and evaluated by those businesses. Theo is always on the lookout for new ways of teaching and new partnerships for innovations. He finds that most of the 300 students he teaches engage actively with the subject at relatively low cost in terms of the input needed from him. He guides them into developing their own innovative approaches. They have become very savvy in using blogs and wikis for help and to support their learning, and Theo encourages them to develop those skills so that they become competent and confident collaborative professionals.

Theo's experience and his rapport with his teaching practice contrasts greatly with Mary's earlier on in this chapter. He finds stimulation and inspiration in engaging in innovative teaching whereas she felt overwhelmed, exhausted and stressed in a working environment that emphasized student-centeredness through a strongly regulated framework, which competed with her own desire to support students in ways that might be recognized as uneconomical. At one level, this suggests that innovation in teaching might be a creative response to the burden of regulation frameworks. It might also uncannily suggest that technology is the answer.

The call for constant outperforming in universities has translated, in the UK especially, into numerous steering initiatives aimed at fostering and rewarding excellence and innovation across the sector (Skelton, 2005, 2007; Brennan, 2007; Gosling and Hannan, 2007). Those incentives are not value neutral. They are generally framed by specific performance-oriented political agendas (Skelton, 2005, 2007; Gosling and Hannan, 2007), and the meaning attributed to excellence or innovation in this context is at best rhetorical (Hannan and Silver, 2000; Clegg, 2007). Those initiatives have often rewarded proposals that privileged the use of technology, the relation to the workplace and the development of work-related skills (Skelton, 2005; Gosling and Hannan, 2007). The race for excellence has been shown to breed competition within departments (Skelton, 2005), privileging forms of practice that are easily amenable to measuring merit, and individuals who are best able to couch their case within a discourse that is recognized by the judges of excellence, thus favouring understandings of teaching and learning as performative practice (Skelton, 2005). The attribution of rewards based on previous records of achievements fails to acknowledge that judgement cannot be detached from the context of practice (Fanghanel, 2007b). Importantly, it contributes to denying the inequalities that exist across universities as it assumes that everyone can become excellent (Skelton, 2007).

Identity and authenticity

The traditional ways of evaluating quality in the academy – based on peer review and professional judgement anchored in disciplinary tenets – are challenged by performativity approaches that emphasize genericism, efficiency and transparency. The threat to academic identities is encapsulated in the fact that academics can be left feeling dispossessed of their expertise and professional judgement (Martin, 1999; Newton, 2000; Ball, 2003). A culture in which recording and measurement of performance come to dominate work rhythms profoundly changes the way academics work and think of themselves as academics. It can turn teachers into 'docile subjects' (Skelton, 2005: 6) as already suggested. There are also positive accommodations of performativity that allow academics to gain recognition for their ability and willingness to engage – in the innovation agenda, for example. Ball (2003), however, has warned of the risk of loss of 'authenticity' in adopting values hitherto alien to the academy, suggesting that new kinds of professionals are fashioned, and new roles endorsed (as champions of performance), which may represent inauthentic commitments. In the same vein, Deem and her colleagues (2007: 200) have detected 'incongruence' of identity as they talked to academics who were affected by 'bilingualism' as they seem to navigate with equal ease both discipline values and neoliberal managerial values.

Performativity carries the dual potential risk that academics internalize performativity habits (Ball, 2000; Walker and Nixon, 2004; Deem et al., 2007) and that collegiality subsides at the expense of 'new forms of institutional affiliation and "community", based upon *corporate* culture' (Ball, 2003: 219) (my emphasis). Suggesting similar lines of potential stratification within academic communities, Deem and colleagues (2007: 201) propose that management may become increasingly 'divorced from the everyday activities and routines of academic knowledge work', and therefore separated from mainstream academics. Normalization of the performativity agenda is a phenomenon that has been challenged, however, in Clegg's (2006) small study of academics in a new university, where such a pattern might be expected to show, and in Trowler's (1998) earlier in-depth study of a similar type of institution. Some researchers, however, have expressed the concern that the language of performativity and rationality is nefariously colonizing the academy as a whole as universities are led into impression management and lose the ability to communicate genuinely (Abbas and McLean, 2003).

Fears have also been expressed that new entrants to the academy who are only familiar with performativity cultures may develop a lopsided view of academic work, and of their role and relationship to students. This is not necessarily the case. Both Mary's and Theo's cases – though only illustrative – suggest that tales of self-actualization, as well as responses of despair and rejection, are possible. The data reported in this chapter also show a complex mix of endorsement and rejection of this agenda. Other chapters will further emphasize the complexity of the responses of academics to neoliberal ideology and provide examples of responses that resist, subvert or re-appropriate it. The multifarious nature of those responses indicates that a quiet and constant project of identity reconstruction is at work in academics' engagement with their practice.

Conclusion

In this chapter, I have shown the impact of managerialist policies on academics in practice, and I have identified work intensification, visualization of work and streamlining of practice as the main emerged facets of this agenda. With reference to interview data, I have examined academics' responses and have established that there are nuances in the positions they adopt towards this agenda. It can be seen as obstructive (coming in the way of the academic values of freedom and trust) or as facilitative of values and practices that enable participation of the many, and allow for democratizing of a hitherto unchallenged right to 'act as one sees fit' by mere virtue of one's academic position. Although managerialist approaches may reflect some form of democratizing, as criteria and judgements are made explicit, the fact that they generate 'fabrications' is real and troublesome. I have also discussed the concepts of excellence and innovation as examples of distant state steering to which some academics were able to relate positively. In sum, I have highlighted as a significant menace for the integrity of the academy the risk of breeding a compliant tribe that could only operate within the parameters of instructions and regulations, and Ball's related warning of the potential danger of a loss of 'authenticity and commitment' (Ball, 2003: 225).

Undeniably, and unsustainably, of those academics I have spoken to who sought to re-introduce authenticity in their practice whilst complying with the requirements of regulation, many were prone to overwork, anxiety and despair. Academics can, however, act reflexively and, in some ways, fashion their roles – their positioning in practice being informed by their own histories, trajectories and ideologies, which provide material to adopt or resist the neoliberal agenda underpinning the practices described in this chapter. This possibility does not fully eliminate the threat to academics' identities from that which wants to 'discipline' them. However, I will show in this book that even those academics who choose to comply with the policies imposed on them do not necessarily buy into the neoliberal agenda; some use it to put into practice, in authentic ways, their own views of higher education.

Chapter 2

Learning to teach in higher education

Introduction

This chapter focuses on early career academics, and more specifically on the moment of practice concerned with learning to teach (LtT) in higher education. Although there are also research development programmes available to academics and researchers in universities, they are not discussed in this chapter. This, to a large extent, reflects the fact that research development programmes are less new and less contested (in respect of their purpose, approach and scope) than are LtT programmes. I consider specifically here the impact on early career academics of formal development programmes that prepare them for teaching and learning. Given the significance and relative novelty of the emphasis on teaching capabilities in universities, it seems fit that a book on being an academic should dedicate a chapter to the teaching development of newcomers to the academy. I consider first the context in which these programmes emerged in the UK and the controversies surrounding their introduction. I then examine the change theories and the theories of knowledge underpinning this form of professional development. In the second part of this chapter, I turn to considering, with reference to formal published evaluations of these programmes, and to my own data, the impact of LtT on early career academics.

Context

There are various possible models for preparing academics to teach in higher education, and I briefly consider mentoring later in this chapter. The United Kingdom, Australia, New Zealand and Northern Europe have developed specific in-service programmes aimed at early career academics. In contrast, most European countries and the United States (D'Andrea and Gosling, 2005: 74) have included preparation for teaching in higher education within doctoral programmes. There is also ongoing continuing professional development provision for experienced academics in most universities. However, the focus of this chapter is on early career academics.

Learning to teach courses were set up in the UK in the late 1990s in the wake of a UK enquiry known as the Dearing Report (NCIHE, 1997), which, at the time, advocated an explicitly neoliberal approach (consumer choice, competitivity, relevance to the economy) to learning, teaching and research. Although various forms of preparation for teaching existed before that in the UK (Trowler *et al.*, 2005), provision for teacher preparation in higher education in the previous two decades had been rather inconsistent, and had tended to be confined to non-university sector higher education institutions whose mission was unequivocally focused on teaching (Cryer, 1981). Programmes for early career academics are being developed worldwide, although their length and content are varied. There is some evidence that Australia, New Zealand and the UK offer programmes for early career academics that have much in common (Kandlbinder and Peseta, 2009). Northern Europe is quite aligned to these trends too (see Roxå and Mårtensson, 2008 for the Swedish case).

The educational programmes designed to prepare academics for their teaching role in universities reflect, to a large extent, the complex agendas discussed in the previous chapters, which have triggered a focus on the relation between higher education and the economy, and generated competitive environments for universities and academics. In the UK these programmes were to a large extent developed under the aegis of the Higher Education Academy (HEA) – a publicly funded organization – previously known as the Institute for Learning and Teaching in Higher Education. A framework of Graduate Certificates (often referred to as 'PGCerts') has emerged across the sector. The HEA accredits today around 160 Graduate Certificates (or equivalent) and 100 lower-level qualifications in the UK. I focus in this chapter on this initiative and start with a vignette illustrating an early career academic's experience.

Vignette three: Patrick learns to teach in higher education

Patrick is a biochemist at a UK university, in a department in which there is a strong emphasis on research. He teaches biochemistry to biology and medical students. As an early career academic, he has been asked to attend a 'learning to teach' programme that is run by the university Teaching and Learning Centre. This programme is attended by academics from across all disciplines to prepare them for teaching, learning and assessment in higher education. At his university, as in many others in the UK, this programme is mandatory and linked to his securing a permanent position after his first three years in post. Patrick was quite keen to get on this course from the start, and quite eager to get what he thought would be some basic guidance for teaching in higher education. On

the course, he quite enjoyed meeting colleagues from outside his department, and being exposed to ways of doing things that were not those of
scientists. He found the programme and the discussions very interesting. The
teaching team always introduced references to research on learning, which
was all new to him. When it came to actually teaching biochemistry to his
students, however, Patrick found that there were very few things he could
apply to his own context. In biochemistry, assessment, for example, revolves
around short answers, longer essays, multiple-choice questions, and that is
about it. So hearing about portfolio assessment, case-based assessment and
co-assessment was very interesting but he did not see how it could be used in
practice. As a junior member in the department, Patrick was not in a position
to influence his colleagues much; and students with whom he had tried one
of the techniques learnt on the teaching course appeared politely amused,
but puzzled. Why was he the only lecturer in the department doing this, they
asked? A lot of what Patrick had learnt on the programme seemed sensible
to enhance learning, a lot of it made sense, but he was the only biochemist
on this university-wide programme; his departmental colleagues were mainly
well-established academics and had no time or inclination for what they saw
as fancy new techniques.

The faculty development team were well aware of how important it is to
link pedagogical theory to the discipline being taught, and they had been run-
ning some seminars in his department about problem-based learning (PBL),
which was increasingly used on science and medical programmes. Those had
been quite interesting sessions. However, Patrick agreed with the rest of his
colleagues that this approach was time-consuming and challenging. They had
decided that, although this was perfectly acceptable for their courses with
medical students, they could not use this resource-intensive method for biology students, who were not, after all, *their* students. As Professor Lee had
rightly pointed out, last year only four out of a possible 120 had ended up
carrying on with biochemistry. So it was legitimate to argue, given the very
large numbers in the first year, that they wouldn't take up such methods. As
he rightly put it, 'it's down to resources really'. Patrick agreed with that. Not
to mention that it does take a lot of time to prepare a PBL course; you have to
make sure you go through all the eventualities because medical students are
quite willing to challenge you and to want to argue a different case – you had
to always be well prepared to try and explain any answers they might come
up with. Patrick thought this mode of teaching was very different; students are
contributing more, but as a tutor you don't feel as in control because it can go
in different directions depending on how they interpret questions. You can try

> and point them in a direction if they've got problems but for a lot of the time they can go off at a tangent. They might come up with the right answer, but they might come round to it using a different approach, so it is all rather stressful ... At least, that was Patrick's view of it.

In this vignette, Patrick's experience as a new academic mandated to complete a programme to develop his teaching skills is typical of that of many. His interest in new techniques, in comparing notes with other colleagues from different disciplines, and his account of the obstacles encountered when trying to implement new ideas in his department is an experience shared by many early career academics in similar situations. When such programmes are mandatory, as in Patrick's case, it is important to bear in mind that, as they learn to teach, these academics are also likely to be engaged in teaching (new and sometimes large courses), competing for research grants, completing a doctorate, designing new courses and fulfilling other academic duties. Early career academics coming from industry and the professions may also be engaged in professional activities outside the university. In addition, they will be dealing with other practical challenges facing any newcomer to an unknown city or a new institution. The burden of practice and the expectations of performance therefore weigh heavily on them.

Ideological and theoretical underpinnings

Introducing LtT programmes *en masse* in the UK, Australia and New Zealand in the late 1990s signalled some considerable formalizing of the relationship between academics and their institutions in terms of conceptualizing teaching expertise. At the time of their introduction in the UK, it sent a minor shockwave through the academic community, which had hitherto remained largely untouched by concerns over teaching competence, and where it was broadly accepted that expertise in a subject conferred sufficient competence to teach it without further qualification. Formal LtT programmes are still regularly the subject of derision in the UK higher education press. Frank Furedi, for example, writing about PGCerts in the UK expressed his contempt in no uncertain terms:

> The very idea of accrediting academics as teachers is fundamentally flawed. It is based on the assumption that there are some generic skills that can be transmitted to the academic. In reality, gaining accreditation as a university lecturer has little to do with becoming a competent teacher. . . . It is about indoctrinating new lecturers into values of a conformist orientation towards teaching . . . It is not possible to accredit an academic's flair and originality. Accreditation is based on ticking boxes and

capturing outcomes. For most academics attendance at these compulsory programmes is an exercise in time-serving and demonstrating an ability to jump through hoops.

(Furedi, 2005, partially cited in Knight, 2006)

This position is predicated on what could be termed a charismatic view of teaching – seen as an innate capacity resting on flair and originality – an exhibition of mastery and knowledge that is not amenable to training or development. There are many such conceptions of teaching amongst academics, which are conveyed by images of the 'sage on the stage' and an emphasis on 'enthusiasm' and 'performance' (Brown and Race, 2002: 55). This fits in neatly with understandings of teaching as a 'vocation' (Weber, 1919) – irreducible to rationality, mastery or logic. By contrast, opting to formalize the preparation of new academics reflects the necessity to learn about learning, the curriculum or technologies (for example) in a mass education system, in order to teach effectively without relying too much on charisma for one's interactions with students. It also reflects some democratizing of the way teacher–student relationships are conceptualized – bringing the sage back to earth, in a manner of speaking. Although these programmes may be useful in providing guidance of the kind Patrick was appreciative of, the limit of what they can achieve has been signalled in various areas of the literature on change and faculty development (Blackwell and Blackmore, 2003; Fanghanel, 2004; D'Andrea and Gosling, 2005; Manathunga, 2006; Kandlbinder and Peseta, 2009). I show in this chapter that LtT programmes remain dislocated from the realities of practice and may fail to deliver change. They are also significantly abstracted from academics' desire to impact differently on their students, through infusing a sense of criticality, broadening the mind or fostering in students 'a will to learn' (Barnett, 2007).

In respect of their change impact, these programmes build on ill-conceived and insufficiently articulated causal theories of change (Trowler *et al.*, 2005), which presuppose that there is a direct relationship between instruction and impact on teaching practice, and perceive of change as contamination. In this model, the more academics attend training programmes, the larger the critical mass of experts and innovative practitioners, and the more likely dissemination and emulation will occur in university departments. This approach assumes that a focus on the micro level of practice (training individuals) automatically improves collective practices without taking sufficient account of local departmental cultures and disciplinary conventions and beliefs that can act as significant barriers to change (Trowler, 2008). A contamination conception of change also fails to take account of the agentic responses of individual academics. I will show below that ideological positioning, pedagogical beliefs and sheer preferences and desires play a significant role in the way that academics behave and relate to their practice and to their students in different moments of practice.

Considering now the epistemic underpinnings of these programmes, a question arises in respect of the dominant paradigm of reflective practice that most endorse, and which is translated in the requirement to submit a teaching portfolio (a collection of reflective work on different aspects of teaching practice). This model was promoted in the UK by the Institute for Learning and Teaching in Higher Education and built upon by the HEA. It reflects an approach to conceptualizing practice that is based on Donald Schön's (1983) proposition that high levels of reflexivity enable practitioners to understand the complexity of professional practice and to operate more efficiently within it. It is a model that is deemed consonant with the need to acknowledge the complexity of professional practice. It is derived from canonical models in medical and nursing education and is considered a more effective way of developing professional practice than would be, for example, a list of competencies. It can be argued that, in principle, reflective practice allows for the surfacing of tacit knowledge and produces conceptualizations of teaching that account for the complexities of practice and evade a model based on technical competencies (Barnett, 1994; Brockbank and McGill, 2000; Eraut, 2000; Moon, 2004). One could therefore suggest that, in theory, it acts as a counterpoise to the performativity understandings of teaching practice discussed in the previous chapter.

Reflective practice is, however, a contested model of professional development. Although it is not within the remit of this chapter to enter deeply into the controversy, I will cite a few of the objections levelled against it. Clegg's (1999) view is that it conveys a craft conception of teaching, as an activity uninformed by theoretical and abstract knowledge. It has also been criticized for reproducing the very rational model of practice that it sought to reject by seeking to generate rational propositions on teaching practice (involving hypothesizing and testing) out of seemingly subjective data (reflective diaries, for example) (Van Manen, 1991; Donnelly, 1999). It has been presented as a mere rhetorical mantra (Ecclestone, 1996), although critical versions of reflective practice have also been promoted (Brookfield, 1995; Parker, 1997). Generally, in the way it is enacted in practice, with its focus on individuals, reflective practice does not acknowledge structural forms of power and collective momentum as significant motors for change. The relativist stance of reflective practice, with its focus on individual practice and self-observation, is disempowering. Rather than providing a powerful response to performativity, it has been described within the Foucauldian framework of self-surveillance as 'a means of social engineering and monitoring of conformism' (Macfarlane and Gourlay, 2009: 458). The focus on 'the journey' (processes) (Macfarlane and Gourlay, 2009) also deflects from the potentialities of intellectual reference to formal abstract knowledge about learning and the curriculum.

Alternatives to LtT programmes

Before going any further into examining LtT programmes, one might want to ask: where would academics learn about teaching if this formal preparation were not available? Peter Knight (2006) has shown that academics' two main sources of learning about teaching are (1) trial and error – just doing the job of teaching – and (2) reproducing or departing from models based on their own experience as students. This raises a number of questions in terms of the efficacy of such methods for generating better learning environments, in particular:

- Do academics reproduce good practice models or do they simply impersonate what they recollect as being good teaching?
- When they relate to negative models, how are they guided in their reflection to devise better models?
- Are their decisions based on evidence or impressions?
- What criteria do they apply in the trial and error process? How does it relate to the practice of the team with whom they teach?
- Can the overall teaching performance of a university be improved through learning on the job?

The list goes on. Self-help techniques clearly have their limitations. To alleviate this, universities have been known to rely on models that involve using the expertise of experienced colleagues to support newcomers. Mentoring schemes (i.e. experienced academics advising early career academics) have for a long time been a common form of academic induction in both British and US universities (Blackwell and McLean, 1996; Cox, 1997). It has been suggested that the arrangements for mentoring are perhaps more structured and better anchored in institutional cultures in the United States than in the United Kingdom (Knight and Trowler, 1999: 33). Whatever its degree of sophistication, mentoring as a form of academic socialization surfaces a number of issues. First, from a purely professional perspective, seniority is not *de facto* synonymous with expertise and knowledgeability; senior academics do not always have adequate formal – informed by theory and research – knowledge of teaching, learning and the curriculum. Second, the limitations of the underpinning contamination theory of change discussed earlier, which assumes that impacting at individual level will filter down to practice, and affect collective progress, stand. In the case of mentoring this theory is at best naïve (as discussed above); at worse, it may simply be perverse – focused on transmitting dogma and expounding the mythical glory of the 'golden era' of the academy (Taylor, 2008), thus preventing early career academics from engaging with new concepts and new ways of doing things. Reliance on experienced colleagues can therefore contribute to maintaining existing practices. Third, power issues involved in a mentor–mentee relationship are not conductive to learning and advancement of practice; specific (personal) mentors' agendas cannot be overlooked. These have been acknowledged, though not entirely debunked, in the literature (Knight and Trowler, 1999; Buchanan *et al.*, 2008). Fourth, mentoring focuses on learning from experience, which maintains – as does reflective practice – a divorce from propositional abstract knowledge about the field.

Knight and Trowler have argued – not unlike Cox – that mentoring should be one aspect only of a broader set of initiatives to socialize early career academics into a specific academic culture. They have suggested that mentoring can meaningfully supplement formal courses (though they do not make specific reference to the LtT courses I am discussing here) and have underlined the importance of local departmental practices, and of the crucial role of the head of department, in this exercise (Knight and Trowler, 1999: 33). They appear, however, to favour 'socialization through daily life' (p. 32), which maintains teaching practice within the bounds of the experiential. From a sociological perspective, one further important question arises, which is also a significant issue in formal LtT programmes: is the knowledge acquired by individuals easily and effectively transferable to daily working practices? I examine these issues now as I probe the impact of LtT programmes through academics' responses to them.

The impact of LtT programmes

Going back to Patrick for a moment, and to his experience of LtT programmes, it is clear that he enjoyed the chance to explore his own context of practice with reference to that of colleagues in other disciplines, and the opportunity to have a space where issues could be discussed with peers in the light of research on teaching and learning. Those are significant advances for faculty development when compared with mentoring schemes or self-help. An important issue in respect to these programmes, however, concerns the translation to practice. Patrick, for example, was unsure about how he could use the ideas discussed on the LtT programme as he was a junior member in his department and felt that he had little power to influence. I now turn to this rather intractable issue of the translation to practice, after a brief incursion into the potential benefits that these programmes can confer, and a brief summary of some formal evaluations in the public domain.

In my conversations with early career academics, individuals reported the following general benefits gained from attending these programmes:

- *Networking*. Being able to share experiences with colleagues from across the university was seen as extremely valuable. It provided opportunities to develop links with other disciplines about both research and teaching; for some, this was also a forum where they could express views that could not be expressed in their own departments – a space of freedom and safety.

- *Skills*. LtT programmes broadened academics' teaching repertory and provided opportunities to rehearse new techniques in a safe (i.e. free from criticism and risk) environment. It gave them a chance to consider practice from the long view; such programmes could almost act as advance organizers – a way of slotting ideas and concepts into categories and frameworks that contribute to better understanding.
- *Understanding of complexity*. LtT programmes delivered by specialists in teaching and learning provide access to abstract and peer-reviewed knowledge that enabled new academics to understand issues they encountered in practice with reference to the research and the theory in the field of teaching and learning. They also began to realize that, although there are a few tricks of the trade, teaching and learning is a complex situated activity – not an exact science.
- *Getting feedback*. Respondents indicated that LtT programmes had contributed to opening the doors of seminars and lecture halls, providing opportunities for peer review and problematizing of practice.
- *Documenting practice*. LtT programmes generally require participants to keep records, diaries of their practice and reflection thereof, often submitted as electronic or paper-based portfolios. Although the limitations of reflective practice have been discussed, as has the performativity dimension inherent in this exercise, developing a style and a means of recording one's practice was seen as a useful professional attribute.
- *Enhancing academic identity*. Some academics reported increased confidence in their own skills and ways of doing things, and increased sophistication in understandings of the relation between teaching and their disciplines, students and learning.
- *Becoming strategic*. Academics who have undertaken LtT programmes can become more aware of the policies and strategies within their institutions, and become themselves more strategic in the way that they organize their teaching, connect with relevant bodies and colleagues, and plan their professional development.

There have been a few studies in the UK formally assessing the impact on practice of LtT programmes. Gibbs and Coffey's (2004: 99) early study of LtT programmes involving twenty-two universities in eight countries pointed to the usefulness of teacher preparation in relation to student learning. It claimed that academics who undertook this formal preparation reported that they were more student-focused than those who did not. Gibbs and Coffey also found that academics obtained better student ratings, and that their students adopted deeper learning approaches. However, in a study examining academics' perceptions of those programmes in eight different institutions from a broader theoretical perspective (formal versus informal learning), Peter Knight reached different conclusions, with an overall emphasis on the significant role of informal learning in practice:

- Professional formation as a teacher in higher education is substantially affected by simply doing the job, one's own experience as a student, non-formal workplace interactions with others, and staff development provision
- Levels of satisfaction with the various ways of developing as a teacher are modest
- There are hints that the benefits of PGC [sic] courses may most strongly disclose themselves some time after completion, especially when graduates are in a position to design or substantially change modules or other aspects of provision.

(Knight, 2006: 5)

Knight contrasted his findings with those of Prosser and his colleagues (2006), who surveyed thirty-two UK institutions and sought to take account of the context in which the programmes were being delivered. Specifically, Knight found he could not corroborate their claim that accredited programmes had a positive impact on teaching and on student learning; or that they were well related to institutions' missions; or that these programmes could have a significant impact at the departmental level – although his respondents mentioned impact at the individual level (Knight, 2006: 37). However, he found his study to be in agreement with Prosser and colleagues' finding that an institution's orientation towards teaching or towards research was a critical factor (p. 37). Given the complexity of teaching practice, and the very different theoretical perspectives adopted by the evaluators, it is perhaps not surprising that formal evaluations of LtT programmes reach contrasting conclusions. Directly linking those programmes to improvement in student learning (Prosser et al., 2006) or change in conceptions of teaching (Gibbs and Coffey, 2004), however, may be making bold linkages. For the purpose of this chapter, which is concerned with the interface of these courses with early career academics, it is useful to keep in mind the benefits that can be drawn by individual participants from formal exposure to research on learning and teaching (Knight, 2006), and the reference to the significance of the institutional stance in both Knight and Prosser and colleagues' evaluations. Discussing the tension between individual benefits and institutional stances leads naturally into an examination of academics' responses to this agenda with reference to the context of practice.

The reality gap

The potential benefits of LtT programmes identified earlier are not felt by all. The impact of the context of practice, and of academics' own beliefs and values, cannot be underestimated when dealing with the notion of becoming an expert academic. Let us consider the following statement about expertise:

One colleague was recounting that he had made an unexceptional remark [in a departmental meeting] talking about engaging with the students when some academic at the back of the room stood up and said '*I am a Professor, that is what I do, I profess. Once the words have left my mouth, I have no further responsibility for them.*'

(LtT Programme Director; my emphasis)

This respondent's quote indirectly illustrates the kind of challenges facing new academics when they return to their departments from sessions on LtT programmes. As junior members, it is often very difficult for them to implement ideas that have been discussed on the LtT programmes and to speak with authority in the face of long-established local traditions, often supported by specific discipline-related beliefs about knowledge, teaching and the curriculum. What I have called the reality gap in this moment of practice is populated with obstacles that prevent direct application to practice of what is learnt about practice on the LtT programmes. I have identified three types of obstacles. The first is of an *epistemic* nature and refers to the difficulty of transferring knowledge from one area of practice to another; the second refers to practical *structural* hindrances, and the third to *ideological* dissonances between that agenda and the beliefs and desires of early career academics. Those obstacles, of course, are not specific to early career academics, but their effect is amplified at this stage as participants develop and shape their identity as academics.

The question of transfer

The view that what is learnt on LtT programmes can be easily transferred to practice is quite simplistic. It assumes a transmissive view of knowledge – understood as content conveyed to learners for direct application to practice – and ignores the complexity of applying it to a different context. Of the many transfer theories that acknowledge cognitive, behavioural and socio-cultural components in the transfer process, the work of activity theorists and social realists such as Young provides particularly useful insights. From an activity theory perspective, Yrjö Engeström (2001) has defined transfer as a crossing of boundaries between two different contexts (or 'activity systems'). He has argued with Terttu Tuomi-Gröhn that teachers should aim to transform learners – the same would apply to teachers who study on LtT programmes – into 'boundary-crossers', equipped with the skills necessary to transit between contexts (Tuomi-Gröhn and Engeström, 2003). At the risk of simplifying their complex argument, this involves collective questioning and probing of existing practice – a kind of analytical deconstruction of prevailing practice to identify and resolve or alleviate tensions between contexts. Strategies to teach the crossing of boundaries include a set of 'actions of expansive learning'

(Tuomi-Gröhn and Engeström, 2003: 31) involving a cycle of questioning, modelling, implementing and reviewing.

Guile and Young (2003: 67) start from the premise that transfer of knowledge in vocational education has assumed either that knowledge can be acquired through experience, or that 'on the job' knowledge can be supplemented by college-based technical knowledge. They state that generally educators have treated abstract and vocational knowledge as falling under the separate responsibility of colleges or employers; or left students to make the connections themselves; or laid emphasis on knowledge in the workplace (situated) to the detriment of codified (abstract) knowledge (p. 79). They propose that all learning includes abstract as well as situated knowledge and emphasize the importance of providing learners with the means to relate codified and situated knowledge from within the curriculum (p. 79) through processes of 'activity development' and horizontal (practical) or vertical (intellectual) 'recontextualization'. Unfortunately, in the context of the LtT programmes examined here, very little communication occurs between the two contexts of practice (the programmes and teaching practice); the programmes often function entirely remotely from disciplinary teams and departments, with little acknowledgement of, let alone work on, existing mismatches, and therefore very few opportunities for either horizontal or vertical 'recontextualization'.

Acknowledging the complexity of transfer provides a powerful explanation of the incapacity in which participants to these programmes find themselves when applying theory to practice. What is missing perhaps from the activity theory framework – mainly because it is not directly applied to thinking about teaching in higher education – but is endemic in the notion of 'vertical recontextualization', is an emphasis on dissonances across disciplinary epistemologies. Certain disciplines find it more difficult than others to relate to LtT programmes whose theoretical underpinnings are mainly grounded in the social or human science (sociology or psychology) disciplines. Transferring to a very different disciplinary context, in which beliefs about knowledge and about the nature of evidence differ greatly, can be a serious obstacle:

> On the whole – this is a horrible stereotype and generalization – but on the whole, engineers aren't comfortable with it . . . They are more comfortable with recipes and if there are any people as a group of which I can say we've achieved the least with, they are probably the engineers. They are not happy, they tend to be more positivistic in their approach, therefore find themselves uncomfortable with the soft and woolly nature of education theory and the lack of clear boundaries.
>
> (LtT Programme Director)

Although this faculty developer is providing an explanation of why teaching and learning knowledge may seem opaque to certain disciplines ('woolly' and not clear-cut), it is fair to accept that such 'positivistic' approaches to knowledge can be explained with reference to the discipline of engineering, or other science-based disciplines. In practice, however, this inability to fully understand complex learning principles can translate into surface application of generic principles, and result in deleterious practices and ill-formed ideas about students' behaviours or attitudes (Fanghanel, 2004). Patrick, in the vignette at the beginning of this chapter, was also quite baffled by the learning theories discussed on the programme. Unlike the engineers referred to above, however, he was able to understand why PBL was an effective learning strategy in his field of biochemistry; the difficulties encountered were of a structural (economic) nature. This is discussed next.

Structural obstacles

Some of the early career academics I have interviewed have indicated that the student-centeredness and constructivist approaches advocated on LtT programmes do not always pass the reality check in practice. Structural local obstacles that come in the way include lack of time, large groups, resource allocations, departmental emphasis on research rather than teaching, requirements from professional bodies and so on. Many such narratives emerged from my discussions with academics. The anecdote below is just one case in point. This chemistry lecturer describes his approach so:

> There is a certain thing to chemistry that you actually need to write it [in order] to learn it; it is like conjugating French verbs.

This respondent feels very strongly about teaching chemical structures through drawing the different ways in which bonds reorganize under certain conditions. He believes that this writing/drawing process is part of the learning process. He is disturbed in his practice by a university policy which states that all handouts should be made available to students through the institutional virtual learning environment platform, in advance of lectures. For him, this is anathema and he firmly believes that this policy hinders his students' learning:

> We now have to put our notes on Blackboard. And that means that students when they come to the lectures have already printed out the notes, they have the notes with them. I am afraid, if I see that I take the notes and rip them up and I insist that they all write, no matter who they are . . . they write during the lectures. Notes are there for them to check. But they believe that just by attendance and looking at the notes they will learn it. And I truly believe that this is completely impossible.

Whatever the value of the theory of learning underpinning his beliefs, this academic's story clearly shows how university policy can interfere with what academics consider best for their students. In the same way, it is difficult for early career academics to transfer knowledge and practice to contexts where long-standing practices prevail, or where values differ greatly, as indicated by this LtT Programme Director:

> We always talk about 'good practice', but when they actually go back into their School [or Faculty], nobody talks about 'good practice'; they talk about research, delivering on research, so that's another thing. Or if the Head of School really does not believe that good teaching matters, or does not send signals that they believe good teaching matters, then the staff generally are not enthused or motivated to feel the same.

Academics with junior status undertaking LtT programmes can influence even less the ways things are done in a department or within a teaching team:

> There are a lot of external constraints and as I am a sort of junior person, I can't say 'well I am going to do it my way' and I couldn't do that.

The power issue works both ways, of course, and some respondents also talked of the assurance they gained from having attended LtT programmes, and of their confidence in trying new things, almost *despite* their more experienced colleagues:

> I think what [the LtT programme] does serve to do is, it causes you to be a little braver. I think it's very easy for experienced colleagues to say 'because I have done this on a number of cycles, this is what I will continue to do' . . . but I think that I am prepared . . . to go in that direction, try that, try new things.

Power and empowerment were also an issue in Patrick's vignette. His status as junior academic gave him little authority to change practices in his department, much less indeed as he did not have any entitlement to affect the complex resource issues, related to the funding formula used in his department. This left Patrick quite frustrated, wondering whether the faculty development team were fully aware of his predicament in his department. On the other hand, his reflections on how teaching (in PBL mode) without a safety net can bring on anxiety and apprehension convey a disquiet that exists in many early career academics, for whom the learning experience of getting to know about teaching can be stressful and challenging (Knight, 2002).

Ideological dissonances

Finally, an important (and relatively understudied) dimension in examining the effects of LtT programmes on academics is that of their own personal beliefs about their role as educators – what they perceive as being their ultimate purpose in their interactions with students. I have outlined the notion of educational ideologies in the introduction chapter and suggested that they permeate all moments of practice. I identified three main ideological orientations: *production* ideologies, which establish a direct link of higher education to the economy; *reproduction* ideologies, anchored in a kind of neo-Humboldtian or Newmanite idea of the university in which learning is conceived of as for its own sake, with an emphasis on the importance of the discipline, and disciplinary enquiry; and *transformation* ideologies, which focus on promoting change for individuals and society.

In the case of early career academics, ideological dissonance occurs when the values underpinning the LtT programmes clash with their own beliefs. Academics holding reproduction ideologies, in which the emphasis is on the subject matter, and the educator's role is conceived of as transmitting a body of knowledge (or a discipline), and the student as a person driven by intrinsic interest in a subject, may find the emphasis on employment-related skills difficult to accept:

> There is a lot of philistinism about, as if universities were indeed there to promote the short term aims of society which are taken to be what? Make us all rich, for what purpose? It is never clear. What do we do when we are all 'richer'? Quote unquote . . . A university should engage on a slightly higher mission.

Academics who hold transformation ideologies, which acknowledge a critical function for higher education, as a structure capable of overturning dominant paradigms, similarly wish to impose on what they do, what they teach, the stamp of transformation, whether this applies to changing individuals:

> I aim to facilitate the creative process with an understanding that their general creative drives are stunted, atrophied, non-exercised through self-doubt, lack of practice, all kinds of things. So it is a major task.

or to impacting more broadly on society:

> Chemistry has a role in educating people to understand the predicament inherent in the city . . . Asthma caused by car exhausts is caused by something invisible which people who aren't trained in thinking about gases, liquids, and so on don't really believe it's there if you can't see it; and every few years the number of children with serious asthma is increasing all the time and eventually you have to admit that in certain cities, like Mexico City or Calcutta, for example, everybody will have asthma. Therefore I feel that a chemical understanding is important. There is a lot of misunderstanding about things.

I have observed elsewhere that ideologies are not monolithic constructs; competing ideologies co-exist within individuals (Fanghanel, 2007a, 2009c). Although academics may exhibit a dominant ideological stance, often their positioning is much more complex (including overlapping competing stances) and episodic (positions varying according to the context in which they operate, or the moment of practice concerned). Their ideological beliefs impact significantly on the way they conceive of students and envisage their interactions with them. This will be discussed in the next chapter.

Conclusion

In this chapter I examined the challenges facing newcomers to the academy with specific reference to LtT programmes developed in the UK and elsewhere to facilitate preparation for teaching. Having discussed the context in which those programmes were developed, and their theoretical underpinnings, I have briefly examined possible alternatives, emphasizing the limitations of seeking to change collective practices through an impact on individuals. I considered then the impact of these programmes in practice through my own data, and formal evaluations of these programmes. I identified some of the benefits academics could gain from exposure to LtT programmes – particularly in respect of becoming acquainted with other ways of practicing in different disciplines; building links with heterogeneous groups; expanding their understanding of teaching and learning; and developing confidence about their own practice. I have also highlighted the limitations of this form of preparation, particularly in respect of the lesser impact associated with programmes that do not take account of transfer issues, or of the structural incongruities and power issues inherent in university environments, or of academics' own beliefs about the role of higher education.

The issues identified in this chapter reflect the challenges of seeking to professionalize a complex academic role. It is unlikely that these challenges can be overcome rapidly, and this chapter in a sense has only provided the premise for a reflection on this moment of practice. At this early stage in my reflection on being an academic, I simply suggest that this relatively new facet of the academic role needs to be re-examined with a view to including it within a framework that is less formal (and accreditation may not be the best outfit), less isolated from departmental and disciplinary realities, and better able to capitalize on the opportunity offered of a broad-ranging critical dialogue that could foster intellectual engagement across institutions. Building on Senge's (1990) idea of a 'learning organization', in which collective thinking informs practices, I suggest that the emphasis ought to be on generating more empowering models to reflect on teaching in higher education, which would not reinforce the hierarchical division within the academy, and which would generate collective powerful knowledge that involves and serves the whole academic community so that rich, learned and dialogic teaching environments can emerge. I suggest that research on one's educational practice (as explored in Chapter 5) might be one of the ways in which to engage early career academics with the complexity of educational practice in a richer, more dialogic manner.

Chapter 3

Conceptions of students and learning

Introduction

The moment of practice examined in this chapter concerns the relation of academics to students and learning, and the way it is conceptualized in higher education policy discourse, and in practice. A strong – and contested – paradigm in today's universities is that of the student as 'consumer' (Streeting and Wise, 2009) or 'customer' (White, 2007). It is a term that has emerged in policy discourse alongside the economic views of higher education discussed in Chapter 1. I show, however, in this chapter that academics and the academy can offer several counterpropositions to this model. Analysing conceptualizations of students and learning both at the macro level of policy discourse in a UK policy text, and at the micro level of academics' own beliefs, uncovers them as multi-dimensional and containing a significant ideological component that relates to the three types of educational ideologies discussed in this book – *production* (an economic function for higher education), *reproduction* (a mission for higher education to maintain its intellectual edge, advance knowledge and validate knowledge claims, and initiate to a discipline) and *transformation* (a broader relation to the individual and the world and a desire to educate for change).

I examine first the discursive discrepancy between the macro level of policy making and the micro level of practice (in an academic's relation to her students) through a vignette that illustrates two opposite conceptions of learning, and of students. The ideology of production and the related view of learning as a commodity are then further explored through analysing the discourse of the UK National Student Survey (NSS). The focus then shifts to the micro level, and academics' conceptions of students and learning. Different counterpositions are identified and discussed. These juxtapositions illustrate the potential inherent in the academy for challenging the dominant consumer paradigm. These alternatives might serve to begin to outline different ways of shaping the complex relation of academics to students and learning.

The focus of this analysis is sociological, and therefore quite unlike studies that have examined the relation between learners and academics through conceptions of learning in which learning is studied as an intellectual process and considered mainly as a cognitive object uncontaminated by political, social and economic constraints. From those psychology-oriented perspectives, there is a significant body of knowledge – from within the phenomenographic tradition, in particular – that has brought to light (with more or less emphasis on the situated nature of learning) the importance of promoting 'deep' learning, and appropriate teaching approaches to facilitate that (Marton and Säljö, 1976; Biggs, 1987; Marton *et al.*, 1993; Prosser and Trigwell, 1999; Trigwell and Ashwin, 2006; Ellis *et al.*, 2008; Yang and Tsai, 2010). From within more resolutely cognitive understandings of learning a significant body of work has also yielded important findings about ways of engaging students in the discipline (Shuell, 1986; McCune, 2004; McCune and Hounsell, 2005; Edmunds and Richardson, 2009; Hounsell and Anderson, 2009) and of fostering epistemic maturity (Baxter Magolda, 2009) so that they firm up their intellectual identities and gain increasingly sophisticated understandings of the nature of knowledge (Perry, 1970). Theorizing the notion of 'alienation', as has Sarah Mann (2001), is also a useful way of examining the relation to students; it is theoretically closer to the approach taken here. This chapter perceives the relation to students and learning as mediated through policies, discourses and the context of practice. These mediations bring the wider societal context into the equation. They also frame teaching and learning in somewhat specific ways – as activities that translate into specific curricula that privilege certain types of knowledge, certain teaching approaches and certain forms of assessment. Although practical curriculum issues are not examined closely here, the ideologies underpinning the curriculum surface in the various student conceptions discussed in this chapter.

The contrasting discourses of policy and practice

In a foreword to an article by academics leading a university centre for undergraduate research (Taylor and Wilding, 2009), the Chief Executive of the UK Quality Assurance Agency wrote:

> Many terms and phrases are used to describe the relationship between universities and students, such as 'consumers', 'active participants', 'co-producers', 'partners', 'community of learning' and 'apprentices'; all are useful, but each has limitations and particular connotations.

In reality, as a result of the neoliberal climate in higher education discussed earlier in this book, the discourse of marketization appears to dominate, and is imbued with a *production* ideology that represents higher education as a commercially competitive gateway to employment. This conception of the student is, however, highly contested by some academics who might display instead a *reproduction* ideology and a desire to educate into a discipline according to the tenets of peer-reviewed knowledge, or a *transformative* orientation in which higher education is seen as having a direct impact on individual or societal transformation. These different beliefs translate into different interpretations of the curriculum, and can affect the way academics approach, for example, the teaching of 'generic attributes' (Jones, 2009), which are used as vehicles for conveying those ideologies.

Vignette four illustrates the discursive rift between two opposing conceptions of the student in higher education. The first conveys a production ideology. It is extracted from a paper by the former UK Secretary of State for Business, Innovation and Skills (the UK Education Department) outlining priorities for higher education. Although highly situated in time, this paper conveys a discourse that is similar in register to that of many policy texts that fall in the 'education reform' package theme (Ball, 2003: 215), and it is unlikely that the form of discourse it conveys will become significantly outmoded in the foreseeable future. The second – adapted from an interview with an academic – suggests a transformation ideology. The juxtaposition serves to expose the tensions resulting from political agendas for academics struggling with the realities of practice, and seeking to uphold their own values. It highlights a sharp division between a discourse of competition grounded in a narrative of efficiency and employability, and one of engagement and intellectual development. To add complexity, those discourses are anchored in totally different contexts, reflecting two different levels of practice – the macro level of the policy maker, and the micro level of the academic in her practical relation to students.

Vignette four: The meaning of learning and teaching in higher education

We will give new priority to the programmes that meet the need for high level skills . . . This will mean enhanced support for the 'STEM' subjects – degrees in the sciences, technology, engineering, and mathematics – and other skills that underwrite this country's competitive advantages. There will be a greater element of competition between universities for funding, with the winners being those universities who can best respond to these evolving economic challenges . . . To allow funds to be diverted to courses that meet strategic skills needs they will be diverted away from institutions whose courses fail to meet high standards of quality or outcome . . . We will bring together universities, employers, HEFCE and the UK Commission for Employment and Skills (UKCES) to identify and tackle specific areas where university supply is not meeting demand for key skills, and will expect all universities to describe how they enhance students' employability. There can be no room in the system for vocational programmes that do not constantly evolve to meet changing business needs ... It is a top concern for business that students should leave university better equipped with a wider range of employability skills. All universities should be expected to demonstrate how their institution prepares its students for employment, including through training in modern workplace skills such as team working, business awareness, and communication skills. This information should help students choose courses that offer the greatest returns in terms of graduate opportunity.

(BIS, 2009: 12–13)

For me the question is always how to bring the sort of conceptual frameworks that I think are important and interesting about changes in the world today, how to get students engaged with that. I think a lot of it is about intervening ... imagining that I might be providing an opening for people to think in a way that is different from other kinds of general ways in which arguments take place in politics, or in the media, or ... I like to give students the latitude to feel that they can develop what they really want to do, allowing them the space to develop their work, their projects. I am often feeling that I completely exhaust myself. I feel that I have a lot of responsibilities as a teacher and my interactions with the students are incredibly important to me and it is necessarily tiring. Good teaching and engagement with the students is tiring. Sometimes students come in for feedback or further tutoring on specific aspects of their course, sometimes they come in with more personal and difficult issues to share. This can take a lot of time, because for me, for example you know a student will come and again. A student will come in, her father was murdered, he is a taxi driver, you know a taxi-cab man, and he was murdered and she is . . . , and her mum doesn't speak English. I know there are services that deal with this in the university. But what do you do when a student comes in like this? And if something like this happens, a student comes to see me, then I am not particularly functional for the rest of the day and similarly with writing, I am not a machine, in either my teaching or my writing.

Although a juxtaposition of this kind is relatively facile, its purpose is to illustrate, beyond the difference in ideologies and conceptions of learning, the gap between policy and practice. One discourse speaks of competition, markets and the economic benefits that higher education is expected to contribute, the necessity for universities to meet the needs of business; the other speaks of space, engagement, passion, exhaustion and tragedy.

The terms 'economic' (eighty-seven occurrences) and 'the economy' (fifty-one occurrences) flood the discourse of the *Higher Ambitions* paper. 'Participation' appears thirty-one times and 'partnership' (often in association with 'business') fifty-one times. The terms 'excellence' and 'excellent' appear sixty-eight times; 'social justice' four times; and 'society' twenty-six times. I have shown in Chapter 1 the insidious collapsing of neoliberal values into the concept of excellence; the policy paper examined here, as a skilled exercise in equating economic relevance with excellence, illustrates how this conflation works discursively. The effect stems not just from the neat balance between the number of occurrences – and the relative imbalance in relation to 'society' and 'social justice' – but from making a convincing case for 'excellence' (in this extract 'the winners') by repeatedly linking this notion to that of 'economic relevance', thus bringing the two terms in a relation of synonymy. Although simple accounting of occurrences is a relatively playful exercise, it conveys a broad sense of the author's preoccupations. The text is authoritative in tone, technical and entirely disconnected from the realities of practice – purely in the realm of policy rhetoric; it provides a set of precepts and prescriptions for universities' strategic engagement with an economically relevant agenda. It carries assertions about the role of higher education that do not call for contestation and do not entertain failure towards those who 'fail to meet standards'. It is a text anchored in taken-for-granted ideological assumptions (universities as hothouses for developing human capital) that apply market principles to higher education without any problematizing.

The second text in contrast uses terms such as 'intervening', 'imagining', 'opening', 'latitude', 'allowing', 'space' and 'engagement', which convey an entirely different perspective on education and learning. It brings in connotations that present learning as a mind-broadening and developmental enterprise – remote, it would appear, from government's preoccupations with the economic agenda. This academic's role is also 'difficult', 'tiring', carrying 'responsibilities' that go well beyond the adequacy of economic supply and demand. The academic is 'not a machine' and 'not particularly functional' in the face of the challenges of practice. The discrepancy between the two texts reflects vividly the inadequacy of market mechanisms to account for what happens on the terrain of practice. This incursion into discursive contrast is not simply a linguistic distraction. In practice, it translates into tensions and problematics that affect academics on a daily basis as they interact with students.

Conceptions of learning in the UK National Student Survey

Seeking to evaluate 'the student experience' – namely the response of students to a complex form of engagement with learning, academics and the wider university community from within very diverse contexts – is not a simple endeavour. Internationally, the higher education sector has been trying to capture this through nationwide surveys such as the National Student Survey in the UK, the National Survey of Student Engagement (NSSE) in the United States or the Australasian Survey of Student Engagement (AUSSE) in Australia and New Zealand. Although the US and Australasian (to a lesser extent) surveys focus on objective measures of engagement, and include questions on motivation and engagement with the learning environment, the UK equivalent aims to collect students' opinions of the quality of their experience.

A recent evaluation of the NSS in the UK has shown that, although the statistical robustness of the instrument was not in doubt, it was not always used by institutions to make valid comparisons; for example to compare whole institutions or to compare courses across different subjects (Ramsden *et al.*, 2010). The focus of my critique is not on how it is being used – however important this might be – but on the principles that underpin it. The NSS envisages the learning experience in ways that focus on learning in the classroom, leaving aside emotional, social and broader contextual and sociological factors, and therefore fails to capture the complexity of the educational experience. The set of twenty-one questions addressing six areas of the student experience and including a final overall impressions question (see Table 3.1) indirectly pass judgement on academics' performance in ways that can be perceived as contestable as they are anonymous and without direct right of reply. More importantly in my view, the conceptions of learning, students and teaching that underpin the questionnaire are resolutely instrumentalist, and oriented towards direct and immediate usefulness for the students. They include elements such as speed, volume, effectiveness and fitness for purpose of the teaching and learning transactions and the needs-satisfying function of the environment. The emphasis is on student choice and perceived measures of their self-improvement. Questions bearing on academics' effectiveness present them as a commodity (a resource) and probe their entertainment value (their enthusiasm, ability to make the subject interesting) and their facilitating skills (being good at explaining). As Macfarlane (2007: 59) has rightly signalled, such a view of teaching emphasizes its 'performance' dimension, and leaves aside the important 'offstage' activities that contribute to student learning. Significantly, no questions in the NSS touch on the broader questions of conceptual development, transformation or intellectual space discussed earlier in the second part of the vignette.

Table 3.1 The values and conceptions of learning underpinning the National Student
Survey (NSS)

NSS questions	Underpinning values and conceptions of learning/higher education (HE)
1. Staff are good at explaining things	Staff as commodity
2. Staff have made the subject interesting	Staff as commodity/entertaining value
3. Staff are enthusiastic about what they are teaching	Staff as commodity/entertaining value
4. The course is intellectually stimulating	Learning as commodity
5. The criteria used in marking have been clear in advance	Effectiveness of teaching–learning transactions
6. Assessment arrangements and marking have been fair	Fitness for purpose of teaching–learning transactions
7. Feedback on my work has been prompt	Focus on speed
8. I have received detailed comments on my work	Focus on volume
9. Feedback on my work has helped me clarify things I did not understand	Fitness for purpose of teaching–learning transactions
10. I have received sufficient advice and support with my studies	Focus on volume
11. I have been able to contact staff when I needed to	Needs-satisfying focus
12. Good advice was available when I needed to make study choices	Needs-satisfying focus
13. The timetable works efficiently as far as my activities are concerned	Effectiveness of provision
14. Any changes in the course or teaching have been communicated effectively	Effectiveness of provision
15. The course is well organized and is running smoothly	Effectiveness of provision
16. The library resources and services are good enough for my needs	Needs-satisfying focus
17. I have been able to access general IT resources when I needed to	Needs-satisfying focus
18. I have been able to access specialized equipment, facilities or rooms when I needed to	Needs-satisfying focus
19. The course has helped me to present myself with confidence	Needs-satisfying focus
20. My communication skills have improved	Fitness for purpose of HE experience
21. As a result of the course, I feel confident in tackling unfamiliar problems	Fitness for purpose of HE experience

The theory of education underpinning this survey is coherent with the performativity agenda explored in Chapter 1 and the related dominant production ideology. It signals conceptions of transmissive models of teaching and learning (learning as an object that can be acquired if channelled through effective staff and resources). It leaves aside any sense of desire and effort, or of learning as underpinned by a complex mix of cognitive and non-cognitive processes and interactions. As one of my respondents amusingly put it, talking about the NSS:

> One ought to feel a bit resentful of the fact that the emphasis is all on the side of making things transparently clear from beginning to end. They would never dream to say 'were there any examples of confusion that turned out to be productive a bit later on'. They would never dream of asking a question like that, nor would I dream of suggesting it. So that is excluded, one has lost something.

The NSS is part of the battery of tools that privilege a consumer view of the student. It is a form of consultation that is presented as a student-centred agenda, whilst setting students in the unfortunate position of passing a judgement on teaching and learning as a product. Initiatives of this nature have in reality formalized rather than diminished the divide between teachers and learners, as they generate different sets of expectations in students, and inflect views of learning that divert students from the desire to learn and academics from the desire to teach *pro bono*. The notion that learning might be a collaborative (Lambert *et al.*, 2007), critical (Barnett, 1997) and engaging activity (Barnett and Coate, 2005) is totally absent. Complexity is removed from the equation. The focus is on material spaces and rational explanations of the learning environment. The emotional and imaginative dimensions that play a part in promoting or inhibiting learning are left untouched; as is the notion that learning is unsettling, uncomfortable at times and not about satisfaction. The view that a curriculum might need to offer properties such as 'fluidity', 'liquidity' or 'instability' and space for students to develop their own 'voice', as Barnett and Coate (2005) suggest, is simply missing. Tangibility and rationality are at the heart of this conception of learning, and of the way the relation between academics and students is conceptualized.

In reality, the production ideology has been promoted in higher education for several decades now, and it is central in accounting for academics' positioning towards students and learning. This ideology holds the dual potential of heavily influencing the way academics operate or of mobilizing energies for resisting it. The conceptions of students and learning examined in the next section – as responses to this dominant paradigm – do not necessarily exhaust all possibilities. In particular, they do not focus on the significant technological dimension – 'generation Y' (digital natives) students (Howe and Strauss, 2000) – or on the 'student as object of study', which has emerged from policies promoting reflection on teaching and action research that often include interviews with students, and analysis of students' feedback. Some of the conceptions I now turn to direct the reflection towards counter-examples to the consumer conception inherent in the NSS. I begin, however, with a further example of conceptions of students as consumers that emerged from my own data.

The student as consumer

Conceptions of the student as a consumer have fostered a focus on performance and satisfaction. Rather than conceptualizing learning as an intrinsically engaging activity, this paradigm emphasizes the utilitarian aspects of education. Relevance to student needs is generally understood as facilitating the delivery of a body of knowledge that will be useful towards employment, often in a context that favours context-dependent and experiential forms of knowledge, as discussed in the introduction. Learning is facilitated through experience and practice, and students are given access to circumstances and methodologies that imitate the real world and seek to develop meta-cognition (learning how to learn) skills that support learning.

The notion of 'curriculum alignment' (Biggs, 2007: 25) discussed in Chapter 1 provides an illustration of what might be a consumer's curriculum. As an abstract rational view of the curriculum it presents learning as a package that is entirely predictable (with a set of intended learning outcomes), and which can be delivered through methods for teaching and assessing that *align* with what the consumer has agreed to buy. The role of the academic is to deliver, and that of students is to play their part to ensure that they succeed. This promotes an 'I pitch, you catch' view of learning that limits the space for exploration and improvisation. The diktat of teaching *to* learning outcomes is humorously conveyed in the following remark from one of my respondents:

> If you ask [students] a question which perhaps involves some knowledge that they have learnt in some other part of the course, they get indignant with us saying 'well we haven't done that with you, we have done that with somebody else in a different course'.

In this paradigm, learning is seen as a commodity in which knowledge is a set of rationally compartmentalized components:

> There is very much this feeling that you do the work, you are tested, and that's the end of it, you close the door on that piece of work, and this is what the students are like coming through now. You can't do that with economics, it builds up, you can't shut the door on your first year and think you are never going to need it again, you can't do the second year without reference to the first year.

Qualifications are reduced to currency:

> We might think students are here because they want an all-round educa-
> tion. That they need an education that can enable them to be more free
> thinkers, critical thinkers, creative thinkers. Students may have the idea
> that it is not really what I am here for, there are other things in my life and
> what I really want out of university is the opportunity to get the degree in
> the time that I have got available in that three year period.

The conception of students as consumers impacts on practices in ways that
are not predictable. Below, one of my respondents explains how such views
(here reportedly held by students) can create tense learning environments:

> In a teaching committee only this last year, one student representative
> said that she'd had one of my students complain to her because I asked
> questions in lectures and this wasn't fair because if you were daydream-
> ing, it woke you up (laughs), or it made you feel like you ought to read
> your lecture notes before coming to the lecture, and she didn't think that
> was fair, this was a lecture after all and you weren't supposed to do work
> for a lecture.

There are also imaginative forms of resistance to the student as consumer,
such as, for example, critical apprenticeship models or introducing intellectually formative content in vocational subjects, which I have discussed elsewhere
(Fanghanel, 2009a). Conceptions of the student as vehicle for social transformation examined later also offer a form of resistance to this dominant model.

The student as deficient

Psychologically, deficiency can be understood as lacking in ability or attributes. Some of the academics I have spoken to perceived of mental faculties as
either being there or not being there. They seemed to hold what Dweck has
called 'entity theory' (1999: 20) – as opposed to 'incremental theory' (p. 20)
– views of intelligence. In other words, they saw intelligence as a given rather
than as an attribute that could be developed. Dweck (1999) has shown how
entity theories could have detrimental effects on students' approaches and
their leaning outcomes. I also showed in previous work (Fanghanel, 2009a)
that this could also have detrimental effects on teaching approaches, with
academics perceiving students' abilities as predetermined, and using methods
aimed at mitigating what they saw as fundamentally lacking – broken-up lectures, short assignments, withdrawing access to notes until after the lectures,
withdrawing support until proof was given that enough individual effort had
been produced, and so on. Examples of deficiency conceptions include:

> You end up with students that frankly shouldn't be here by any normal standards, if it wasn't for political or economic pressure, and then you have to worry about retention, so you spend so much effort to pull students through a system where you seriously – if you stepped back from what you are doing – would start having doubts about whether it is even good for them to go through this.

Views of students being lazy, or not trying hard enough, belong in the same type of conceptualization, although the evidence to support this belief is missing:

> But the thing is here, somehow, students expect things, but they are not . . . they are not ready to put in their effort much which I find a bit frustrating. You know if somebody comes to me and asks for help, and I can see that this person has struggled for maybe even twenty minutes with the problem and got sort of stuck, I love to help them, it's fun . . . If a student comes to me and asks 'what shall I do here?', I ask 'here is the problem, have you read it?' 'Yeah.' 'Where are your lecture notes?' 'Here.' 'Ok, how about you look through to see which part of the lecture notes might actually be pertinent to that problem?' I am not paid to tell them these things . . . I am not there to tell them 'look at your lecture notes.'

From a sociological perspective, however, deficiency focuses on inequalities generated through some wanting in cultural, social or economic capital (Bourdieu and Passeron, 1977), and on the role of schooling in reproducing those inequalities to limit social mobility. In practice, it translates into views of students as lacking in basic skills, and the necessity to provide some corrective input to remedy this deficit. 'Deficit theories' have been presented – in a critical race theory perspective – as privileging a view of knowledge that is white and middle class, and endorsing knowledge and skills that are valued by that privileged class (Yosso, 2005), disregarding (and therefore failing to harness) other forms of capital that might be inherent in belonging in a non-hegemonic group – for example 'linguistic' capital (ability to speak several languages), 'navigational' capital (the ability to 'manoeuvre through social institutions') or 'familial' capital (values, heritage and attitudes fostered in families).

In practice, conceptions of the student as deficient permeate understandings of learning. Notions of participation and diversity that do not problematize the causes of inequality, and invoke essentializing identity scripts (i.e. social or geographical provenance as an explanation for performance), do just that:

> I do not know if that [widening participation] is necessarily good for everyone and it worries me that people feel pressurized to go into higher education, or feel that their career prospects or their lives are not going to be worthwhile if they have not done it.

The question of whether higher education is actually for all refers to what Nussbaum (2003: 341) has shown to be, in the context of women's literacy development in India, a form of 'romanticizing' and 'monolithizing' of non-literate (or non-hegemonic) cultures. Based on the notion of the 'noble savage' (the nobility and beauty of nature untainted by nurturing), such approaches – in the case of Nussbaum's study, the apology of oral traditions – imply an acceptance of difference and inequality at face value. It perpetuates patterns of 'misery and injustice' (p. 341), in seemingly good faith.

The same deficiency principles can translate – in the context of teaching international students – into views of international students as other, dismissing the notion that home students and academics might also learn from international students. Totalizing prejudices about cultural difference that mark western pedagogical principles as the norm then result in presenting any exogenous approach as deficient:

> Occasionally we come across students who dislike the problem-based learning process and occasionally it tends to be students who come from the Far East and I think perhaps there may be a cultural thing in academia or sort of traditional academia in the Far East where it is completely didactic – this may be changing now, I do not know – but they occasionally have complained that they feel there is just not enough you know . . . because of the fees they are paying here, there is a sense that they see going to a lecture and having someone talk to them for an hour you know . . . that's the education, that is what they are paying for.

Those conceptions do not always translate into open prejudice about the type of students that attend university but they normalize views of teaching as facilitative:

> In the past, you just thought it was the student's responsibility [to learn] because they were capable, it was their responsibility. I think now there is quite a high responsibility on the person educating them to make sure that they understand what they are supposed to be doing because they don't necessarily have the background and the skills to do it.

The student as becoming

Although this student conception also envisages students as incomplete, in contrast to deficiency conceptions it emphasizes the student as a being in the making, and the role of the tutor as engaging with this becoming:

> [Teaching in higher education] was my first exposure to thinking about how do people learn and their paradigms get overturned – what happens in higher education, how the students transform . . . how their world-views get sort of shifted around.

Epistemic development and induction into the tenets of a discipline are components of what a reproduction-oriented academic seeks to achieve with her students. The nature of the relationship to students (building up capacity for the next generation of intellectuals, new discipline specialists) can include seeing the student as a disciple – that is, a relationship in which hierarchy is assumed as part of a legitimizing process facilitating entry into a discipline and higher thinking. The quote below illustrates the mentoring pattern it can generate, here in a rather lord-of-the-manor approach:

> In chemistry you have time to walk around over the course of maybe a whole day in the laboratory and you can talk to the students, explain how their experiment works, and what they are trying to achieve in this experiment, but you get to know the students better, you get to know them on a first name, personal terms, and to know about their personality, so I enjoy being in the lab.

A strong value in this conception – which reflects the frustrations felt about student laziness identified earlier – is that hard work and effort are part of the journey:

> What really gives me lots of pleasure is when a student comes to me and has found it hard to come to terms with a concept or a method of calculation. At some point, through guidance, you actually hear when he finally comes through, there is like a little spark there and when you enable the student to get this sort of epiphany, you see they've made a jump here, they have had a certain amount of success, then suddenly there is something that moves them forward to go on to other things, I think that is really the nice thing about teaching.

In reproduction conceptualizations of the student, there is an assumption that students understand the 'invisible pedagogy' (Bernstein, 1997) – that is, they know that social reproduction, and reproduction of values, are implicitly part of the educational experience, beyond mere access to knowledge.

The hierarchical nature of the relation to students inherent in the illustrations given so far is not always emphasized. Models of partnership have also emerged, in particular under the influence of student-centred active pedagogies. They are part of a wide (but not widespread) move towards engaging students in deciding on learning outcomes and some of the content of their programmes of study. Recent initiatives aimed at enhancing the linkage between research and teaching have, for example, enabled interpretations of this relation as supporting undergraduate research. From those, conceptions of the student 'co-learner' (Healey and Jenkins, 2009), 'collaborator' (Taylor and Wilding, 2009), 'producer' (Neary and Winn, 2009) or 'co-producer' (McCulloch, 2009) have emerged:

If it is acknowledged that both teachers and students are engaged in the activity of knowledge development, dissemination and application, then the current wide gap between teaching and research begins to narrow and, for the undergraduate, learning involves explicit engagement with knowledge and the processes by which it is produced.

(McCulloch, 2009: 178)

This approach is based on models developed in US research universities, in particular as an outcome of the Boyer Commission's (1998) report, which emphasized the importance of research-based learning in undergraduate education. There is a strong ideological intention behind the Boyer Commission agenda, which is to perpetuate reproduction models, and emphasize the difference from what is offered in community colleges (Fanghanel, 2007c). The Boyer Commission model has, however, been appropriated in the UK by teaching-oriented institutions to suggest that linking research and teaching, and engaging students in research, improves student employability (Healey and Jenkins, 2009: 73). In this version, the idea of involving students in research reflects a view of research that focuses on the process, and seeks to contest elitist conceptions. This approach has privileged forms of engagement in which students undertake and publish research with academics, present at academic conferences or are included in research proposals. It is an approach that has, however, been looked upon with a degree of scorn or disbelief by a number of mainstream academics (Taylor and Wilding, 2009) and which remains marginal in its challenging of the 'hierarchical binaries between teaching and research, and teachers and students' (Lambert *et al.*, 2007: 534).

From a more philosophical perspective, and almost as a leitmotiv to his most recent corpus of work, Ronald Barnett has been promoting the 'ontological' dimension of the curriculum – with an emphasis on developing the student as human being and providing space for individual emancipation to enable students to occupy a space where critique and creativity are developed (Barnett, 1997, 2000, 2007; Barnett and Coate, 2005). This displacement implies approaches to teaching that promote student-centeredness and conceptual change almost by effacement of academic authority (Barnett, 2000). The individual, not the collective, becomes the site of emancipation. All these conceptions of the student are strong counterpoints to the view of students as consumers. They remain focused on the individual, however, and are not directly concerned with the more structural views of emancipation developed below.

The student as vehicle for social transformation

A sense that higher education should contribute to developing critical views of a 'supercomplex' (Barnett, 2000) world – that is, a world where criteria and parameters to understand and evaluate are themselves complex – has enduring appeal in the academy. Critical education theory that sets out to emphasize the connection between power and knowledge, and to question and redress the role of education in perpetuating inequalities (Young, 1971; Apple, 1993, 1995; Freire, 1996; Darder, 2002; Allen and Ainley, 2007), and feminist and critical race theories (Darder, 2003; Yosso, 2005) provide a strong basis to support transformative conceptions of students and learning. It is not possible to do justice to the enormous body of work on critical education in this chapter. Suffice to say that it has generated and informed views of academics as transformative educators. It has also impacted – theoretically at least – on pedagogical methodologies, which have increasingly focused on knowledge co-construction and active involvement of learners in the curriculum. Although critical educators' focus is on the role that education can play in redressing social and economic inequalities, there can be some overlap with the issue of employability. One of my respondents claiming, for example, that 'higher education takes kids off the streets' by providing them with the potential to find decent employment, out of the poverty trap where they were raised, is an illustration of this overlap.

In the same transformative perspective, the increasingly significant focus on global citizenship in higher education (Apple *et al.*, 2005; Andreotti, 2008; Bourn, 2008, 2009) has provided a conceptual link for conceiving of students as global citizens. Global citizenship is, however, a fuzzy and contested concept, which spans from approaches that include internationalization of higher education, cultural diversity, global governance, globalization challenges and social inequalities right through to activism, climate change and sustainability issues. The development of 'capabilities' in students to enable them to transform themselves and the societies in which they live (Nussbaum, 2000; Unterhalter, 2003, 2005; Walker and Nixon, 2004; Walker, 2006), mentioned in the introduction chapter, is worth pausing on for a moment. Briefly, the capabilities approach has focused on ways of enhancing human development generally, in all aspects of a person's life. It provides a normative framework and an agenda in the form of 'capabilities' (see Walker, 2006, based on Nussbaum, 2000, for a full listing) that higher education ought to promote. Those include practical reason, educational resilience, knowledge and imagination, learning dispositions, social relations and networks, respect, imagination and bodily integrity. The impact-oriented dimension of the capabilities framework makes it particularly relevant to higher education in emerging economies, to which it refers extensively.

Forms of critical global citizenship that question, beyond the normative activist agenda of the capabilities framework, the nature of difference have also started to appear in higher education discourse. This work questions essentializing identity scripts and focuses on differences within – as well as outside – seemingly homogeneous cultural groups. As an example, Andreotti's work on critical literacy provides an alternative to production and reproduction models:

Critical literacy is not about 'unveiling' the 'truth' for the learners, but about providing the space for them to reflect on their context and their own and others' epistemological and ontological assumptions: how we came to think/be/feel/act the way we do and the implications of our systems of belief in local/global terms in relation to power, social relationships and the distribution of labour and resources.

(Andreotti, 2006: 49)

Problematizing identity in ways that question relativist (i.e. unbridled multiculturalism) as well as westernizing (i.e. insidious monoculturalism) understandings of difference provides a powerful critique of the simplistic dominant understandings of diversity in higher education. These pedagogical approaches relate to the broader notion of worldly becoming that I discuss in Chapter 6 with reference to globalization, and which explores the way that the academy can harness the potential brought about by globalization to engage in shaping understandings of how to live with uncertainty and 'supercomplexity'.

In sum, reproduction and transformation ideologies and the conceptions of the student they evoke reflect academics' perceptions of their mission as contributing to the education of tomorrow's generation of discipline specialists, or of citizens who will apprehend the world from a position of informed criticality. In practice, however, the social transformation models examined here remain circumscribed to the fringes of the academy, and serve more as heuristics to re-imagine the relation to students than as descriptors of mainstream approaches.

The student as recipient of the desire to teach

Thinking of the university as a place of learning and dialogue is something that keeps many academics engaged in their role as educator. As evident in the academic's views in the vignette at the beginning of this chapter, the pleasure and satisfaction gained from interacting with students is important, and accounts to a large extent for the fact that the academic career is perceived as desirable. Desire is a significant driver in accounting for academics' engagement in teaching, regardless of their ultimate ideological aim. Desire is often associated with challenge, as indicated by one of my respondents:

Many of them [the students] will sit there thinking 'why am I here, I don't really want to do this', and it's a real challenge to fire their enthusiasm and make them want to come back to the next lecture, and so this is a challenge and I enjoy it. In some ways it is very much like being an actor on a stage, you stand in front of an audience and you have to perform, and sometimes your performance is good, and the students learn and they are interested and maybe other times, your performance isn't quite as good, the students aren't grabbed by that lecture. You can never rest on your laurels – every lecture, you have to give a performance.

The desire on the part of academics to procure safety and hospitality – identified by Mann (2001: 18) as significant in combating student alienation from higher education – can be quite overwhelming:

> In the first few weeks of the first year I just always feel terrified. Is anything happening? Are they hating it? So there is a fear that if they really hate it, then maybe they will leave and then I will feel responsible somehow . . . I think that I feel most confident if I have built up a rapport with students. When I don't feel that I know how to judge what either one or several students are feeling or wanting, that makes me feel much more anxious.

The passion for teaching and being good at it can translate into anxiety and frustration when the academic feels that she is not succeeding:

> I had a German student who wrote to me on the module report last year, 'don't worry so much about the students that don't want to learn'. Because I get really frustrated by students who are not performing . . . They are not attending, they are not preparing, and you know and I try to do things for them and I set up extra sessions.

Expressions of this desire can also conjure up scenes of an almost Socratic nature:

> I quite like it when I have about ten or a dozen students – not too many – and I can teach them in a sort of seminar sort of way and I am asking questions and they are talking back and then they ask questions of each other and they ask questions of me, and we all talk, and there is some sort of sense of point . . . You know . . . the talking.

The desire to teach students can be curbed by the necessity to be realistic about what can be achieved. In the conversations I have had with academics, this desire often collided with the requirements of the practice – the need to be research productive, the need to confine oneself to a defined set of learning outcomes and the need to comply with what is required within that agenda:

> You are buzzing with ideas with the teaching on how you can make it better. But you have to draw a line and say, 'well, I don't have time to do that' and for all that extra time it would need to introduce that new idea, how much extra benefit is there really going to be?

Conclusion

This chapter has highlighted some important characteristics of conceptions of the student in higher education, and the resulting complexity of the nature of the relation of academics to students. First, through discursive analysis in the vignette, it has emphasized the contested terrain on which conceptions come to life, collocating two contrasting discourses that represent ideologies operating at two different levels of practice. The first conveyed an abstract, authoritative, policy-anchored view of the student as consumer, and higher education as a marketplace delivering educational products that serve the economy. The second was enacted in the locus of practice, and emphasized the pragmatic and emotive character of translations of conceptions to practice; it also outlined a transformation ideology contrasting with that of the policy maker. In the second part of the chapter, I have shown that conceptions of the student are multiple. The conceptions examined here are in no way a comprehensive account, although they are significant in respect of the diverse ideologies they convey and the set of possibilities they outline. Although they do not represent 'ideal types', some of the conceptions of students examined here that depart from the student as consumer either are aspirational (normative), or remain at the margins of the academy. I suggest, however, that they can provide inspiration towards forms of pedagogies that procure an opportunity for engagement with students, and through this, and beyond, with the world in its complexity. In a space where understandings of teaching and learning are generally confined to abstract de-contextualized renditions, it is important to harness the potential of conceptions of students and learning that go beyond the instrumental to engage fully with the meaning of the educational enterprise, and of its relation of the wider world. These broader conceptions allow for different imaginings of learning, and of the relation between students and academics.

Chapter 4

The discipline

Introduction

This chapter focuses on a pivotal moment of practice by examining the engagement of academics with their discipline. Although the increased emphasis in higher education on transferable skills and context-dependent knowledge discussed earlier may have been seen as precipitating the 'decline' of disciplines (Welch, 2005: 3), there is evidence that the discipline remains a strong locus for academic identity (Becher, 1989; Trow, 1994; Henkel, 2000; Becher and Trowler, 2001; Kreber, 2009). The idea of belonging in a discipline and in a disciplinary community is deeply anchored in the academic psyche. Love for one's discipline and the desire to share that passion with students are perceived as significant attributes of a successful academic (Ballantyne *et al.*, 1997). The relation of academics to the 'invisible college' (Halsey and Trow, 1971) of disciplinary collaborators has increased not just with the progress of communication technologies, but also through policy steerings that have encouraged the expansion of international collaborative research. Finally, the discipline is also a crucial articulation between research and teaching in higher education.

After discussing the status of the discipline in universities, I give a brief overview of ways in which the discipline has been conceptualized in the literature. I then turn to academics' own constructions of the discipline, using data that interrogated this moment of practice. I emphasize specifically the way academics' conceptions cohere with the beliefs and understandings of the wider world they bring with them in the academic space. An acknowledgement of the agentic stance brought by academics to their practice, which circulates throughout this book, was discussed in earlier work with specific reference to the way ideology shapes conceptions of the discipline (Fanghanel, 2009c).

The status of the discipline in the academy

In her subtle study of academic identities, Mary Henkel (2000) has emphasized the significance of the discipline in the making of an academic's identity.

Her study, which was published at the turn of the century, focused on traditional scientific, social scientific and humanity-based disciplines, and included a majority of research-oriented institutions. It concluded that the traditional values and a sense of 'academic exceptionalism' (the academic profession being different from any other) were still well alive in the academy (Henkel, 2000: 257). She was able to outline boundaries and differences between discipline traditions, and concluded that, in spite of the many changes affecting higher education, the underlying narrative was 'a story biased towards stability rather than change' (p. 265). She noted that 'academic idealism' (a passion for the discipline, and the desire to communicate this to students) was a strong component of academic identity (p. 56). Her study, in many ways, corroborated the findings in Becher's (1989) seminal study of academics in the 1980s, which also emphasized the discipline as central to academic identity, and to delineating the shape of academic 'territories', and the nature of academic 'tribes'. In a sense, these findings concerning the significant role of the discipline in the make-up of academic identities contribute to legitimizing territorial boundaries and conventions adopted by specific disciplinary groups. They focus on coherence within, and difference without. Although they constitute solid evidence on the role of the discipline in the academic landscape, they tend to present disciplinary identities as more cohesive than studies at a more situated level of analysis (i.e. in the context of practice) suggest (e.g. Trowler, 2008; Fanghanel, 2009c), as I will show in this chapter.

In the past three decades or so, the discipline has come under attack from within and from outside the academy, mainly as a result of interrogations about the nature of knowledge, and of a problematizing of the relation of universities to the wider world, discussed earlier in this book. In practice, the emergence in the late 1970s of curricula emphasizing socio-cultural relevance (Welch, 2005) and the emergence of 'fields' in higher education (e.g. women's studies, literary studies, biological sciences) have largely contributed to an inflection towards multi-disciplinarity, social relevance and preoccupations such as social justice, multiculturalism, gender and social equity. At the same time, post-modern relativist understandings of knowledge have also challenged the epistemological paradigms underpinning the organization of disciplines as fields of knowledge. In parallel, the 'economizing of education' (Ozga, 2000: 24) and the input of professionals in the curriculum has steadily contributed to generating curricula that focus on educating students beyond purely disciplinary bounds – developing 'transferable skills' and 'contextualized' curricula (Muller, 2009). The challenge of these trends to academic disciplines, and to their organization in coherent epistemic groupings, is obvious. Previously discussed calls from social realist theorists for resisting vocationalization and the dominant emphasis on context-dependent knowledge (Wheelahan, 2007, 2009; Young, 2008; Muller, 2009) have, however, sought to re-assert the significance of the discipline, and the legitimacy of its boundaries. These contestations signal a refining and a redefining of disciplinary epistemological underpinnings. I discuss those below as part of an overview of how the discipline has been conceptualized in the literature, after a brief aside on the complex nature of discipline conceptions.

In the course of my discussions with academics, I came to realize that their discipline conceptions were constructed – and possibly, as Taylor (2008: 30) suggests about the make-up of identities, 'continuously "under construction"' – through their own beliefs and histories, and their ideological take on the broader aims of higher education. Thus, I have met academics teaching the same disciplines, in the same institutions or in institutions with similar missions, who displayed entirely different understandings and conceptions of the same discipline. Psychology, for example, was seen as an almost dissident discipline in the medical curriculum, where it was perceived as teaching medical students 'bedside manners' (e.g. ways of understanding and dealing with emotions). In contrast, it was perceived as relatively value-free – conveying objective historically grounded evolutive theories of the mind – in a regular psychology undergraduate programme. In the same way, I have found academics holding very similar conceptions of their discipline in very different institutions – confirming Becher's and Henkel's view that the institution is not as strong an identifier for academics as is the discipline. I also came across a few academics for whom the discipline was not a central focus of their enterprise. One geographer in particular – whom I have cited elsewhere (Fanghanel, 2009c) – indicated that she did not feel any particular 'ties' to her discipline. Her concern was about developing criticality and presenting alternative views of the world, not 'to turn out good geographers'. Before I examine the details of these situated conceptions, I turn to a brief overview of how the discipline has been apprehended in the literature.

The discipline as epistemological entity

Much of the literature on the discipline focuses on its epistemological make-up (knowledge structures, knowledge validation, nature of proof, etc.), and on the related epistemic coherence of disciplinary groups organized around these structures. In this literature (Becher, 1989; Donald, 1995, 2002, 2009; Henkel, 2000, 2005; Neumann, 2001; Neumann et al., 2002; Hounsell and Anderson, 2009) disciplines are described as representing relatively coherent bodies of knowledge and communities of practice. Donald (2009) and Hounsell and Anderson (2009), for example, have suggested that there are ways of thinking that are specific to certain disciplines. This research has also established that specific disciplinary communities have evolved specific methodologies in respect of the way they teach (Shulman, 2005) and research (Becher, 1989) their discipline.

This body of work privileges a focus on disciplines' epistemological properties, generally with reference to Kuhn's (1970) work on which Biglan (1973) based his well-known classification of the disciplines. This classification is itself a distant inheritor of the original distinction in mediaeval universities between the arts and humanities (the Trivium) on the one hand, and the sciences (the Quadrivrium) on the other. It theorizes these distinctions within a matrix that classifies knowledge characteristics alongside two sets of properties – 'hard–soft' and 'pure–applied' – and makes the following distinctions between disciplines (Biglan, 1973):

- hard pure disciplines, e.g. astronomy, chemistry, mathematics, physics, microbiology;
- hard applied disciplines, e.g. engineering, economics, computer science;
- soft pure disciplines, e.g. English, history, philosophy, sociology, anthropology;
- soft applied disciplines, e.g. education, foreign languages, nursing, accounting.

When forms of knowledge are examined from within this structuralist paradigm, researchers have been able to draw conclusions as to the nature of knowledge in the disciplines. They have observed, for example, that knowledge is more certain in science-based disciplines, and more uncertain and unstable in arts, humanities or social sciences subjects; and that this generates more or less 'restricted' research agendas for academics (Henkel, 2000: 190). They have also established that knowledge acquisition proceeds through 'cumulative growth' in hard subjects, and in more organic ways in soft ones (Becher, 1989: 13). The literature has also examined how these epistemic structures impact on teaching and research approaches (Henkel, 2000, 2005; Neumann, 2001; Lindblom-Ylänne et al., 2006; Donald, 2009), student development (McCune and Hounsell, 2005; Hounsell and Anderson, 2009) and learning (Donald, 2009). This way of examining the discipline through its epistemic structures has internal logic and validity. However, there are other dimensions of the discipline that are particularly salient once one looks at disciplines in context, to which I now turn.

The relation of disciplines to institutions and departments

Leaving aside the epistemological focus, a few studies, introducing prestige and class-related elements in their analyses, have examined the role of the institution, and observed how certain disciplines co-locate with certain institutions (Halsey, 1982; Clark, 1987). Clark's (1987: 61) 'institutional–disciplinary matrix' showed, for example, how, in the United States, patterns of distribution could be identified in which scientific disciplines tended to concentrate in high-status research institutions whereas less prestigious teaching colleges attracted softer disciplines. He observed that in prestigious institutions 'disciplinary and institutional cultures converged in a fundamental way' (p. 111), whereas both disciplinary and institutional identification faded in lesser institutions, where the focus on teaching became more important (pp. 111–118). Halsey's work compared long-established UK universities (Oxford and Cambridge) with those established in the 1960s. He concluded that older institutions focused on pure disciplines, whereas newer ones tended to attract applied disciplines (Halsey, 1982: 221). Unlike Henkel, both Clark and Halsey pointed to the institution as a foundational locus for academic identification – Clark emphasizing disciplinary prestige in US universities, and Halsey relating this phenomenon to class factors in the UK (Halsey, 1982: 222). Although these studies are quite dated, their emphasis on the institution remains valid and informative in any sociologically minded account of the disciplines, especially as increased stratification of the sector since those observations were made has further determined disciplinary specialization.

A number of studies have shown the crucial role of the department in mediating disciplines' 'demands and desires' (Clark, 1987: 64), and its influential role in defining the nature of what is being researched (Clark, 1987; Henkel, 2000, 2005) and taught (Clark, 1987; Trowler, 2008). Henkel (2000: 253) has found, for example, that academics relate better to their department than to their institution, and that the department can become a site of 'collective opposition' to the institution, which academics view mostly as 'limiting their control of the working environment'. Although indeed, by tradition, the academic home may have been – and may still be in some cases – the department, other forms of disciplinary units have emerged: specialist groups within departments, discipline-specific groups in large multi-disciplinary units, research groups, for example. Some universities still have relatively cohesive single-discipline departments. Increasingly, however, as universities re-structure, a number of large multi-disciplinary units have also appeared. Within them, teams that tend to operate independently from each other exist as quasi-autonomous subunits or fields. These formations are defined by their disciplinary characteristics, the cultural features of their work environment and the group members themselves. Their commitment to a group, as identities in action, is inflected by pragmatic considerations – timetables, co-teaching of modules, teaching innovation projects, for example. Trowler, who has carefully studied this level of practice with specific reference to local 'work groups' engaged in teaching and learning, using the specific notion of 'teaching and learning regimes', has rightly observed that analysis at this situated level of practice unveils complexity:

> As the level of analysis moves from an aerial view to one closer to the ground it is clear that . . . broad generalisations begin to lose their coherence; the picture becomes more complex. Thus other categories of difference acquire significance and the boundaries between them increasingly dissolve.
>
> (Trowler, 2008: 11)

The department is a space of turbulence where individuals, groups and structures interact intimately; and where academics collaborate and compete in equal measure. As a result, currents of influence in and out of the department impact on how academics understand their local practice (Fanghanel, 2009b; Roxå and Mårtensson, 2009).

Disciplinary cultures

Becher was one of the first researchers to emphasize the social characteristics of a discipline. He examined the connection between the discipline as an abstract set of structures and its instantiation in individuals and communities. He spoke convincingly of the particular characteristics of specific disciplinary communities. This led him to observe that academics' specific working practices result from the 'fundamentally different intellectual challenges' they encounter (Becher, 1989: 281), bringing to the fore differences between disciplines and discipline idiosyncrasies. He talked of 'recognizable identities' and 'particular cultural attributes' (p. 22), making up 'tribes' who have their own 'heroic myths', their own disciplinary discourse and artefacts:

> a chemist's desk is prone to display three-dimensional models of complex molecular structures, an anthropologist's walls are commonly adorned with colourful tapestries and enlarged photographic prints of beautiful black people, while a mathematician may boost no more than a chalk-board scribbled over with algebraic symbols.
>
> (Becher, 1989: 23)

Becher noted that both the cognitive and the social dimension are 'inextricably connected' and difficult to disconnect from each other (p. 20). Although stating that the epistemological properties of a discipline are not immutable, he envisaged the connection as one in which the cognitive influences the social (p. 4). In the revised edition this assumption on the flow of influence is more nuanced (Becher and Trowler, 2001: 33).

Importantly, informed by theory that has highlighted the polymorphic nature of culture (Alvesson, 2002) and the crucial role played by 'interpretations' in organizational cultures (Tierney, 1987; Alvesson, 2002), the focus on cultures serves to emphasize their non-monolithic nature. Institutions and departments are not coherent structural wholes harbouring well-defined and well-bounded entities. Although institutional reputation and priorities matter at a high level of analysis, there is some risk of 'totalizing' institutional cultures – that is, endorsing the meaning of culture 'in a too all-embracing way' (Alvesson, 2002: 188). Institutions are made up of a constellation of local (departmental) cultures that are very influential in inflecting the shaping of academic identity. Local cultures themselves are not of one piece; tensions, divisions and alliances all affect their make-up. Becher's (1989: 42) work showed the fuzziness at the edges of disciplinary boundaries, and the limitations (untidiness) in using the discipline as a unit of analysis. Trowler's (1998, 2008) work on academic cultures has further emphasized fragmentation, turbulence and dynamism, and drawn attention to some constructed element in the way that disciplines are defined. Looking at the discipline from the perspective of ideological positionings as I do next, the subtle elements that contribute to conceptions of the discipline in the context of practice emerge more vividly. This analysis dents slightly the tale of coherence and unity that comes through at the macro-structural level of analysis. Epistemological cohesion and tribal homogeneity become frayed when the discipline is examined on the ground of practice.

Academics' conceptions of their discipline

I would like to introduce a geological image at this stage to convey the situated and organic nature of disciplinary conceptions at this micro level of practice. Epistemological and structuralist conceptions of the disciplines provide well-defined, strong and relatively stable canonical renditions of disciplines. Geologically, those would look like some crystalline rock, or some piece of ice; they represent reified apprehensions of the discipline. As they become exercised in the context of practice, these conceptions take on different properties and characteristics. Individuals, groups, circumstances contribute to shaping them. Agency comes into play. Geologically, those representations would look like sand on the beach, or mud – soft, malleable and moving. At the micro level of analysis, with the specific focus on ideological inflections, because they are more fluid, these conceptions are also less easy to label, and quite permeable to contiguous ideologies. This translates into understandings of the discipline that can be quite idiosyncratic, as illustrated in the vignette below.

Vignette five: Tony and Jane's conceptualization of English literature

Tony and Jane teach nineteenth-century English literature in two different UK universities – both are research-intensive medium-size institutions. Tony came to teaching literature by the direct route, after completion of a PhD. He developed a taste for literature very early on in his childhood, and is fascinated by the beauty of well-constructed texts. He has two main goals when teaching English literature to undergraduate students. The first is to convey and generate in his students a curiosity and a passion for literature that will last throughout their lifetime. The second is to communicate an understanding of what makes a text work, and a sentence chime. He spends a lot of time examining the texts on the programme very closely, deconstructing with students areas of text to make them aware of the beauty, resonances and harmonies within and across a corpus of texts. He uses software and images to help students understand what makes a good story, a well-rounded plot and a credible character. If he can convey a sense of awe and amazement towards canonical texts, Tony feels that he has been successful in teaching English literature. He is seeking to bring his students in close proximity of beautiful texts, and to promote in them a deep understanding of the first principles that make a text work, rather than to emphasize mere recall of plot and quotes. He does this by making his lectures relevant to students' life experiences, and by providing striking examples and illustrations. He believes mastering the fabric of a good text provides students with the desire to read more, and with the intellectual ease and confidence needed to succeed in later life.

Jane came to teaching after completion of a PhD, following a brief incursion into journalism, and two short-term internships in two prestigious universities in the UK and abroad. She thinks literature is a window on the world. Her main intention when she teaches literature is to develop in her students a critical mind so that they see literature as an account of humanity's questionings and a critique of the taken-for-granted. She thinks the main aim of higher education is to provide a broad critical outlook on the world, and is convinced that English literature lends itself particularly well to this. She wants to be sure that students understand what is really at stake in the texts they read – the political, social or gender issues behind the plot – and that they develop critical views on contemporary issues from their work on those texts. She thinks English literature is a perfect vehicle to enhance political awareness, develop critical stances towards views espoused in the media, for example, and contributes to generating graduates who will stand out in society as critical agents. She is particularly concerned that they use their skills to be critical of what they find on the Internet, in the media or on social networking sites. To do this, she uses the web, multimedia and text adaptations, and she works on deconstructing plots with students so that they read the political and economic agendas beyond them. She is less concerned with developing students' mastery of stylistic norms than she is with their ability to translate their understandings to the real world as a way of shoring up their criticality.

In this vignette Tony and Jane both focus on the same educational aim of making sure students understand rather than regurgitate their subject, but their underpinning intentions are very unlike. From a *reproduction* paradigm, Tony hopes to stimulate a passion for the subject commensurate with his own, and sees his role as producing the next generation of teachers or writers. He sees literature as a wonderful intellectual object; and written works as examples of harmony and perfection. Jane aims for something totally different. From her *transformation* perspective, she seeks to inculcate in her students a critical stance towards the world – reading the press critically, seeing the hidden agendas, understanding and acting on the world through the exposure they get from literature. Similar ideological positionings were present in the conceptions of academics I interviewed on this topic, to which I now turn.

Reproduction ideology: a focus on epistemological structures and induction into the discipline

It almost comes to one naturally to imagine reproduction ideologies to be preponderant amongst traditional disciplines (literature, history, chemistry or physics, for example). This in itself feeds the powerful narrative embedded in the structuralist and epistemological accounts of the discipline discussed earlier. To shore up this intuition, I will cite a classicist I spoke to who exemplified this orientation. His main focus when describing his discipline was on acquaintance with a body of knowledge and transmission of a cultural heritage:

> I have always been interested in . . . committed to opening up, relating – I hate compartments – relating one aspect of experience to another aspect of experience. So decades ago, I was trying to encourage classics students to relate what they were doing in the sense of reading ancient texts, reading texts in Greek and Latin to alternative intellectual ways of thinking – whether fashionable now or not.

He did not want to be seen to be teaching students 'facts and figures' (grammar, vocabulary, dates, authors):

> I cannot imagine what it's like to be working in a subject where it's taken as a kind of principle that what you teach is facts. I indeed don't quite know what that means.

His ultimate goal was through the teaching of classics:

> to bring the individual into relation with this [the western] cultural continuity, if only to challenge it.

A passionate desire to acquaint students with the discipline, and the resultant focus on a body of knowledge and set of values perceived to be inherent in the discipline, characterize reproduction approaches. These approaches do not always reside, however, within traditional disciplines, as in the case of this classicist. An academic who was teaching digital art also felt very strongly about transmission of values and knowledge that linked back to a cultural history. He saw his discipline as 'ambiguously' located on a spectrum that accommodated both its commercial and its artistic properties. He held on fast to the artistic thread. In practice, he played on this ambiguity to position his discipline in the university as an artistic subject, underplaying – and yet paradoxically foregrounding when necessary – the practical skills it could yield:

> I had to argue that ours is an arts-based discipline, [the university] didn't think they had any left and digital art is a weird pathway within the subject which is quite firmly entrenched into the fine arts discipline. So we like to argue for generic applications of it, rather than it being purely vocational. But nicely we can point towards the ICT-related computer skills in giving life skills.

As an educator, he appropriated the artistic dimension of the discipline, and focused on this aspect. He tried to convey to his students the relation to the arts, and to play down the technology. He did that by using arts-based forms of teaching and assessment, including the famous 'crit' exercise. He felt strongly that he wanted his students to develop their creativity, at the expense of the rules and regulations at times, and spoke quite disparagingly of colleagues and students who focused on technical prowess. As master of a discipline, he saw his role in an educationally traditional light, favouring teacher-centred approaches:

> The guru-led approach of the art school where you are following a tutor, trying to find your own practice . . . you are struggling to find your own practice, maybe you are having your own practice destroyed through critique. It's harsh but quite an interesting way to view artistic practice.

This ideological reproduction position was not, however, of one piece. Inside the university, he emphasized the artistic dimension as he thought that gave him, and his discipline, status. Outside, however, he was keen to emphasize the role of the technology, and talked of the tensions this created:

> I have turned into a geek over the past four years, more so than before, so my obsession with technology is part of the dialectic within it and I think that's something that the commentators at Tate Modern [a large UK modern art gallery], they are not particularly dialectical, they think art isn't anything to do with technology. You have to speak to them about the science of paint and then they change their perspective. But the anti-digital, the anti- . . . the . . . Luddite . . . I am using a harsh word – they are not necessarily Luddites. But there are acknowledged technological processes within any form of art.

His ultimate educational aim was:

> to facilitate the creative process with an understanding that [their] general creative drives are stunted, atrophied, non-exercised through self-doubt, lack of practice, all kinds of things. So it is a major task to facilitate creative responses to hopefully self-generated material, so that they provide their own trigger, if not, to provide basic triggers to help them stimulate the creative process.

The case related here encapsulates at the same time the imprints of a reproduction ideology, and the complexity and fragmenting of that position. This digital arts lecturer uses the epistemic binaries in his discipline to navigate the geography of practice – his position as teacher clearly traditional; as a researcher, clearly rebellious towards traditional approaches to art and defending the value of technology; and as an academic manager, totally pragmatic – playing, as he said, on ambiguity to get what he wants.

Production ideology: a focus on application and preparing for the world of work

A production ideology, as discussed in earlier chapters, has increasingly explicitly permeated the academy and the curriculum to compete with other understandings of the purpose of higher education. Production conceptions of the discipline may dominate in vocational subjects, and this may not be surprising. However, there are nuances there too. Of the academics I have encountered who broadly embrace the economic and vocational agenda, a number described what I have called elsewhere models of 'critical apprenticeship' (Fanghanel, 2009a), which included engaging students in some kind of creativity, a critical stance and an ability to contest and better understand the world.

To illustrate, I will take the case of a human resources management (HRM) academic I interviewed whose conception of her discipline was complex within the production ideology. She taught undergraduates in a teaching-oriented university in the UK, and was keen to ensure that her teaching was relevant to the students and to their professional interests; to that effect her main concern was that her discipline should always be contextualized and linked to the professional preoccupations of students and the needs of the industry. She saw it as her main role to equip students with generic skills rather than with disciplinary content:

> It is really the student's job to get the content; it is your job to help them. You are not teaching in the old sense you are more of a facilitator. That's the real two things. So teaching is more about developing people's learning experience.

She felt strongly that her discipline should be taught in a way that is relevant to the profession, with a view to improving standards, and had always objected to seeing her department move to the Business School, which she found too theoretically inclined 'because . . . they don't contextualize'.

At the same time, she also thought that 'there is a necessity to balance the vocational needs of the industry with some idea of broadening people's horizons'. She had therefore included topics that develop students' views of work, and of social, cultural and gender issues in the curriculum. She also saw promoting values such as respect for other people's points of view as incumbent to her approach. Clearly, her conception of HRM as an applied discipline was not about a narrow application of occupational skills to specific contexts.

In theory, a production ideology, as it makes explicit its intention to be relevant to economic interests, can seriously undermine the discipline – and it could be argued that it is only through clinging to some complex ideological positioning, as in the above example, that academics rescue their discipline from that potential elision, and reclaim some academic territory. In some of the academics I met, however, the disciplinary dimension appeared to have faded entirely. I want to turn for a moment to examples of cases in which the discipline was clearly underplayed either as an intellectual and critical entity, or even as a professionalizing concept. Perhaps as a foreboding insight into what a complete victory of the economic agenda, in its literal interpretation, might mean, a few of the academics I spoke to focused solely on the credentializing value of their subject – its exchange value. The discipline, then, became simply a producer of symbolic capital, a vehicle for status enhancement. One nursing lecturer, for example, presented her curriculum mainly as a set of procedures and stated that she was not 'teaching' her students, but 'giv[ing] them situations to play with so that they can see the difference between [practice and study]'. She was preparing her students for practice, and her focus was on professional application. One might argue that the discipline ceases to be a discipline when it is perceived simply as a utility.

An information science academic I interviewed also emphatically spoke of the credentializing function of her discipline, by comparing it favourably with a profession that was generally considered as of lesser status – that of librarians. She stated that she had struggled a long time in her mind with the notion that 'librarians were slightly inferior creatures to information scientists'. She thought that it was through engaging with another discipline, and thus attenuating her own, that the professional identity and symbolic capital of the information scientist was enhanced:

> [Students] have their own subject matter which gives them a professional authority, they are not just scurrying around when somebody asks them for something. I mean we are a service profession . . . but we have a professional authority that says I have subject knowledge.

This position may not be unrelated to the more general issue of the predicament of 'service' positions in universities:

> When I started, it was mainly a woman's job. All service professions, woman can do them. Because we have now so much more IT, now that's not the case, we have more males and the male–female balance is still more women than men but there are more men coming to it.

It seemed that, through some kind of vampire-like process, the reliance on another discipline provided substance to her own; it brought content into what might otherwise be perceived as a skills-only subject:

> You do need a subject. So OK, you have a subject background of some sort and then what we try and give is this idea of being able to estimate the quality of information. Anybody can now use Google and get masses of stuff, but what should they be reading? What is good? So estimating the quality of information, trying to organize the most relevant resources for any query, and therefore still standing as an intermediary between the user and the information.

This academic's conception of her discipline is complex. She displayed a production understanding of her discipline in seeking to develop in students skills that would allow them to become authoritative professionals and focused on the credentials brought by her discipline. The transformational dimension that would provide professional empowerment, however, occurred at the expense of her discipline, which could exist only through another. I examine now understandings of the discipline that foreground a transformation ideology from within the discipline.

Transformation ideology: the discipline as social critique and transformation

I reproduce here extracts of a conversation with a UK chemist whose own biography, academic trajectory and vision of higher education were intricately entangled with his conception of chemistry as a critical discipline that could play a significant role in educating students to transform society. This academic was a first-generation entrant into higher education; his father had worked in a steel-making furnace in the north-east of England. He believed strongly that higher education had a function in changing the world order:

> You've got these people who are not participating in society; I feel this is a shame because that's where I come from. I come from the under-class, I come from a council estate, and I feel there is a lot of talent. Talent doesn't come where you expect it, the country needs the talent. You might miss out on an Einstein, and that makes a big difference. Then, one or two

of them recruiting from the under-class will destabilize that feeling that none of us around here ever get anywhere.

For this chemist, the purpose of a university education was not just to provide students with skills and knowledge for employment, but also with a critical view of the world. He thought chemistry could give students that critical mind: 'Yes, looking behind what is, and see what the reality is, I would say that is the most important thing you can do'. This academic's conception of chemistry was pregnant with this ideological drive:

> I oppose unquestioning acceptance, like if you go to Marks & Spencer's [a UK high street retailer] all the tomatoes are the same size, that is very strange, people are not the same size, why are they the same size? Or if you have certain things that have an enormous shelf-life, what are they doing to these natural things to produce this? So you can apply it to many things where you are as a consumer – you are given things which are produced to make profit, so they add sugar and salt so that the profit is increased. But whether or not salt or sugar is good for the people who eat it, that's not their problem. The sugar and salt are added for the sole purpose of making Tesco [another UK retailer] more profitable. So it takes a strong mind, a questioning mind, but it is a mind that you can get from chemistry if you understand what it does and what is involved in all these things. It can make you a much more difficult customer and a sort of person who is not accepting the way things are dished out.

Interestingly, this critical agenda was perfectly compatible for him with his production stance on work-related skills, which he thought were extremely important:

> I am interested in transferable skills and I want to teach them how to run a computer, how to analyse a problem, how to look things up in a library, how to find information. It's something that I am interested in really. So they have to write in English, they have to record what they have observed, they have to work out how to ask a question, and find out how to set up a system that will give an answer to that question.

This chemist is therefore very much in favour of policies that encourage broadening access to higher education. He organized summer schools for underprivileged school children, and enacted his political agenda through his role as an academic:

> Confronting ignorance is the purpose of education. So you're confronting it all different levels, in the widening participation, you're confronting it in the X estate and you are trying to convince people that if they confront it, they all . . . they can do things.

We see in this academic's conception of chemistry a coming together of complex ideological positions. He presents chemistry as a critical discipline that can help change the world; it includes social and intellectual critique that might be inherent in a transformation ideology, but also strong adherence to the economic agenda, and a production, employment-related agenda.

In summary, exploring conceptions of the discipline in practice, at the micro level of individual academics, provides a perspective which differs from studies that have focused on disciplinary differences between epistemological structures and properties or the role and make-up of a disciplinary group. It allows for ideological and pragmatic dimensions to surface. It brings into play individuals' personal take on the discipline: their perceptions as relatively autonomous agents within a disciplinary community, and in unique relation to the students and the curriculum they teach. Although some disciplines are more relevant to industry than others, and some more anchored in social issues than others, this examination of the disciplines has shown that industry-related disciplines could also be seen as vehicles for social critique. In the case of applied subjects such as HRM, vocationalism could also be perceived as carrying an intellectually broadening dimension. As indicated earlier, much of the specific emphasis is brought by individual academics. Some will focus on the epistemological dimension more than others, refusing to bring disciplinary knowledge into the realm of the profane; others will do the exact opposite – as did the chemist above. Ideologies are enacted in subtle and varied ways. The stance adopted by any academic is rarely absolute or entirely impermeable to other ideologies. The angle of analysis adopted in this chapter – examining the discipline *in situ* – allows for a nuancing of positions on the discipline, and a departure from the epistemic and structural differentials explored at the beginning of this chapter.

Conclusion

I have examined in this chapter various ways in which the discipline can be conceptualized. I have suggested that epistemological and structuralist understandings of the discipline provide a useful explanatory framework at an abstract level of apprehension, but do not fully represent what is happening in the context of practice. Although I have recognized the importance of the disciplinary dimension in an academic identity, I have also indicated that I had come across academics for whom the teaching of a specific discipline mattered less than the general ideas and critical approaches they might develop in their students. In those academics, the discipline took backstage; their own ideology, front of stage. Some also had little sense of belonging in a disciplinary community and appeared to be enacting their discipline as outsiders, focusing on meta-cognition, or resorting to another discipline to advance their own.

I have argued that conceptions of the disciplines are more than abstract epistemological constructs, or structural entities. At the micro level of how

individuals conceptualize their discipline, I have highlighted the importance
of the broader ideological beliefs academics bring with them. This analytical approach takes account of academics' beliefs about knowledge, the world
and the role of education in society; and of their desires and aspirations as
educators. It can be argued – and has been suggested by Barnett and Di
Napoli (2008) – that more complex views of academic identities need to
be imagined. The emphasis on plurality of voices that I have been able to
articulate through the analytical lens I chose to examine the discipline should
be welcome. It signals that the academy can problematize its relation to the
wider world and dialogically accommodate its complexity. Introducing apprehensions of the discipline that are not just structural and epistemic in nature,
but account for ideological and pragmatic constructions, thus contributes to
this re-imagining of academic identities. It also conceptualizes the discipline
as a lively paradigmatic entity that is shaped by the flux of events, discoveries,
societal evolution, ethical positionings and so on. In this perspective, conceptions of the discipline are constantly rekindled as the relation to the wider
world is re-appraised.

Chapter 5

Being a researcher in higher education

Introduction

The research space has been affected, much as teaching has, by performativity, managerialism and the focus on economic returns discussed in previous chapters. In this moment of practice, the neoliberal agenda stands at odds with ideals of discovery, enquiry and intellectual advancement that academics may attach to the research endeavour. Engineering of research priorities through focused (economically and socially relevant) funding opportunities has framed the research space, and the options available for academic research. This has created a highly competitive context in which academics vie for increasingly bespoke research funding.

This chapter focuses on research modes (ways of doing research) and on the potential for articulating alternative modes of research in universities. I first outline the context that has shaped the research field in universities. I then examine the impact of performativity and managerialism on academics with reference to what I have called managed research, as it resonates with issues related to the management of teaching and learning discussed in Chapter 1. Broadly, managed research is funded research that is produced towards publication in peer-reviewed disciplinary journals or reports to state departments or funding bodies. It directly affects national and international rankings and individual and institutional prestige. Managed research is funded through competitive private or public funds and responds to an understanding of research that is increasingly focused on impact factors and socio-economic or social relevance. It has come to determine what officially counts as valued research in today's universities. I show in this chapter that the managed research space is highly structural, with little scope for academics to roam free. In the final section of this chapter, through an analysis of what I have called scholarship on higher education practice (broadly research on teaching and learning practice), I reflect on ways of developing models of research that might humanize and democratize this moment of practice. Humanizing implies modes of research that take into account the human (social, moral or political) dimension of enquiry, as opposed to focusing on value-free (i.e.

detached, objective) knowledge; democratizing involves ways of engaging with non-experts, and of disseminating through public and dialogic forums.

Given its focus on modes of research in the academy, this chapter omits a number of important areas of enquiry. Specifically, it does not offer a thorough review of the research field, and of the many disciplines, traditions, methodologies and ethic codes within it. Nor does it examine the intellectual risks associated with focused research funding and the contribution of private sponsors. It addresses only indirectly the question of the decline of scientific authority (in contested debates about climate change, biodiversity or genetic diseases, for example) through its reflection on democratizing the research space. It alludes to but does not fully exhaust issues related to researcher autonomy, competition of diverse knowledge forms, epistemic hierarchies in the academy and the management of research.

A researcher's profile

Vignette six: Bernard's approach to research

Bernard is professor of mechanical engineering in a research-intensive UK institution. He has an extensive research profile in displacement machine design. He has received many distinctions for his engineering work, and has published well over 200 articles in academic engineering journals. He has taught in higher education for a number of years and has been involved in many large-scale international collaborative research projects. He has extensive research links with colleagues in Eastern Europe and has led a number of engineering design research projects in this part of the world. At his home university, Bernard is very keen to involve both his and his European colleagues' students in his research.

To enable his outward-looking approach, Bernard uses technology as a matter of course. Familiarity with technology gives his students opportunities to work in transnational teams and at a distance, which, Bernard believes, will turn them into globally competent engineering designers. A couple of years ago, Bernard decided to design a model of virtual enterprise that involved five universities in five different countries, and about eighty students. He evaluated his programme throughout the duration of the course, using student feedback to make changes that improved the interface and the learning experience of his students. He also included industry partners in the evaluation. One discrete element of his study bore on the web tools used for communications.

Bernard then made formal presentations about this work in virtual networks and at conferences, and published some of his work in engineering educational journals. Looking back on this exercise, Bernard realizes that, quite apart from the obvious benefits to students, he gained a lot from involving employers in the research and the assessment of student work and from being able to disseminate the outcomes of this experience. This has stimulated the interest of colleagues in other parts of the world, who are now developing courses building on this model. A number of ethical and practical issues concerning engineering in a global world have also arisen from those discussions and Bernard has recently included in his programme charitable and voluntary organizations supporting global engineering development. He has planned some research placements linked to development projects in Africa for next year. This will open up new avenues for collaborative research and bring his students ever closer to solving problems in the real world.

This vignette provides an example of what is perceived by many as an unusual (and perhaps unenvied) academic profile. Bernard is successfully engaged both in disciplinary managed research and in scholarship on his teaching practice; he has managed to link the two forms of enquiry in ways that appear almost natural – certainly harmonious. His scholarship work on teaching is not what is generally understood as research in universities, although there are world-class researchers, particularly in the United States, who see enquiry on teaching and learning as a worthwhile intellectual pursuit and intrinsic to their academic role. I will return to this in the latter part of this chapter as I examine this mode of research – which is not widespread in the academy – to trigger a reflection on its potential for developing the academic research space more generally. The case of Bernard allows me to introduce from the outset a sense that research is not a well-bounded term or a consensual object; competing modes of research co-exist in this moment of practice. The relation of research to teaching, and the tensions this generates, add to the turbulence as, in this relation, research has significant value as scientific capital, and carries more symbolic power within the academy than the teaching (and service) functions (Bourdieu, 1990).

Trends in the research space in universities

Universities increasingly accommodate many modes of research in their midst. This, in the words of Peter Scott (2009: xiii), has resulted in a 'puzzling paradox'. He suggests that research has become at the same time structurally 'more sharply delineated' or 'harder shelled' through funding, management, organizational structures and more clearly defined career paths; and also more 'diffuse' as 'the boundaries between science and technology, scholarship and teaching (and learning), research and enterprise have become more open'

(p. xiii). I use the term 'multimodal' to render this diffusion. Although managed research may be considered more prestigious, research in the academy comes in different guises, and trades under different names, which include scholarship, knowledge transfer, consultancy, practice-based research and even – somewhat paradoxically – practice (see the Centre for Practice as Research in the Arts, University of Chester, UK). This diversity stems from a number of factors, which I discuss briefly below, that are socio-historical and epistemological in nature, but were also driven by specific policy steerings. From an ideological perspective, this diversity also signals interrogations on the purpose of research, and the relation of the researcher to the outside world. In accord with Scott, I suggest that secession from the managed model is at work – albeit perhaps in a peripheral form – in today's universities, as alternative modes of research are emerging.

To examine what potentialities these emerging modes might bring with them, I resort to a cluster of works that have opened new ways of thinking about research. I turn first to Callon and his colleagues (2001: 135), who have argued that, given the complex and contested debates on natural and social phenomena in a global world, researchers need to harness social and technical uncertainties through 'dialogic democracy'. To do this, they must break away from 'secluded' (laboratory-based) forms of research and develop democratic 'wild' research modes (taking account of all stakeholders and of the messiness of the real world). This research must be produced in 'hybrid forums' that are not just interdisciplinary or interprofessional, but are also driven by interactions and debates between laypersons and specialists. This, Callon and colleagues suggest, encourages forms of research that do not take for granted 'scientific authority' but rather seek to reach consensus through informed collective debate and promote 'controversy as a mode of exploration' (p. 28). Alongside the work of Latour (2010), who argues for an examination of science in its connection to social and political interests, they suggest that there is a need to invent new organizational patterns for research, and fair and transparent ways of researching collective problems, in order to sustainably and democratically 'compose' the material world. I also draw on Arjun Appadurai's reservations about 'value-free' (disengaged) research (Appadurai, 2000: 11), Barnett's reflections on the nature and purpose of the university (Barnett, 2005, 2007, 2011; Barnett and Di Napoli, 2008) and Macfarlane's reflection on the centrality of values to the academic endeavour (Macfarlane, 2004, 2009). My reflection is also informed by Barnett's idea that knowledge of the world is always provisional and contestable, and therefore generative of further uncertainty – what he calls Mode 3 knowledge (Barnett, 2004: 251). These provide a substantive backdrop to the interrogations of this chapter; and an emphasis on the values and processes that might need to be taken into account in a re-imagining of the research space outside of the competitive framework of managed research.

The shaping of the research field

The attachment of research to universities is relatively recent; the mediaeval university was a place of learning, not a site for research (Kerr, 1963; King, 2004; Lucas, 2006). Its main function was to prepare future generations of clergy, the emphasis being on 'the transmission of unchanging revealed truth' (King, 2004: 3). It would gradually become a place of training for government employees, public officials, lawyers and doctors, the emphasis therefore still on learning, not on research. It is the German model created by Humboldt at the University of Berlin at the turn of the nineteenth century that would inflect the model of the modern enquiring university, and an appropriation of the research function by universities. Enlightenment and rationality provided the perfect secular sequel to the university's monastic origins. Even if, as suggested by Delanty (2008: 129), this model may have been 'a myth even in its own days', it carries a strong ideological resonance within the academy; it is a model that is emulated, for example, by emerging economies who seek to move away from the 'peripheries' of the research territories (Altbach, 2007) and make their mark in world rankings. This German influence did not lead to the emergence of a univocal model. In the UK, for example, mid-century, Newman (1852) introduced an 'idea of the university' that focused more on intellectual development than on knowledge creation – teaching more than research. A number of countries in Europe had located research outside the universities. This is particularly true in France, where Napoleon had ensured that specialist disciplinary communities were segregated (Paradeise and Lichtenberger, 2009) and separate from high-level professional education (Vatin and Vernet, 2009).

Quite apart from this socio-historical evolution of the research space, theorizing about the process of knowledge creation and the nature of knowledge in relation to different disciplines played a significant role in differentiating the field and inflecting different research modes. Closer alignment of interests between universities, industry and governments (Etzkowitz, 2008) and the requirements of increased contextualizing and knowledge interdependencies (Gibbons *et al.*, 1994) have triggered complex, hybrid and interdisciplinary modes of research. Gibbons and his colleagues, in their discussion of Mode 2 knowledge, theorized this trend by proposing a research model that moved away from the academy into the real world, where transdisciplinary teams work on highly contextualized socio-economic problems to produce knowledge that is socially and economically relevant. As a result of these epistemological shifts, today's dominant research model in the sciences and social sciences is one in which researchers work in highly specialized, hybrid and multi-skilled, often transnational, teams.

The way that different disciplines apprehend knowledge also offers a powerful explanatory framework to account for different research modes (Becher, 1989). Specific methods and paradigms attach themselves to specific disciplines. The epistemic relation to reasoning, proof and truth, for example, is profoundly anchored in disciplinary differences, as discussed in the previous chapter, and accounts to a large extent for the multiplicity of methodologies in research. The rise of new disciplines in the 1970s that extended disciplines into interdisciplinary fields emerged from a questioning of structuralist epistemologies, and brought their own methodological and theoretical frameworks to the table. As university disciplinary fields have become more fragmented, questioning about the nature of knowledge, contestation of knowledge and the relation to the wider world has intensified both within and across subject areas; and modes of research have multiplied. These complex epistemological developments have generated some significant questionings of an ethical nature about the role of research, the relation of the researcher to her object of research and the interference of utilitarian aims with the academic endeavour.

Multimodality of research has also been engineered through strategic management of research outputs, in response to economic imperatives and market forces. A culture combining competitivity and the requirement to address social and economic problems and to demonstrate impact (or benefit) has driven research into specific (generally applied) areas of enquiry, and encouraged national and international collaborations. The emphasis on application, interdisciplinarity and usefulness has promoted specific forms of research engagement. Activities such as small- and large-scale case studies, and consultancy work in the industry, often labelled 'knowledge transfer' activities, have increasingly come into the fold of a university's research portfolio. At the same time, and significantly in the UK, academics have also been encouraged to develop their knowledge base on teaching and learning, alongside their disciplinary research. Thus, an academic such as Bernard in the vignette may have a world-class reputation for his engineering research, and also engage in scholarship on his practice. I argue later, whilst acknowledging that this is also a contested field, that scholarship on higher education practice – unlike the 'learning to teach' programmes discussed in Chapter 2 – has successfully begun to bring into the research field a new form of reflexivity that offers the potential to think about research differently. At this stage of the discussion, however, it is worth noting that this multimodality has created its own hierarchies, with some modes of research and some research outlets being perceived as more worthy than others, and some institutions more likely to generate certain types of research than others. Those structural hierarchies are rarely overcome in practice, and I will show, as I examine the choices made by academics on the ground, that, although they can deploy some agency in respect of some research choices, when it comes to managed research, choices are on the whole made for them, rather than by them. To sum up, this brief incursion into the different modes of research has emphasized the roles played by socio-historical and epistemological factors, as well as the direct impact of policies and research management strategies, in shaping the research field.

Issues in managed research

The impact of managerialism and performativity regimes on universities (and the measurement of research outputs inherent in them) has been extensively examined in the literature (e.g. Slaughter and Leslie, 1997; Naidoo, 2005; Lucas, 2006; Deem *et al.*, 2007; Brew and Lucas, 2009). This body of work has commented on their effect on the morale and identities of academics and on student recruitment, faculty appointments and institutional reputations. It underscored the tendency to accentuate what is known as the Matthew effect – providing for those who already have. In this competitive context, universities have learnt to play to their own strengths and have deployed strategies to ruthlessly harness the research game (Lucas, 2006; Marginson, 2007). This is particularly the case in countries such as Australia and the United Kingdom, where competitivity regimes are at a more mature stage of development, but also increasingly in mainland Europe (Berry, 2009; Chamayou, 2009; Longo, 2009) as universities realize the dangers of losing their competitive position (Descombes, 2009). There is a sense of inevitability in the academy about institutional hierarchies. Even if newer more teaching-oriented universities are forced to play the research game (King, 2004), stratification in terms of reputation and opportunities is stark. On the field of research, the game is unequal.

Although institutions may enjoy a degree of autonomy in how they manage research as they adapt and interpret state directives (Musselin, 2009), the agency of individuals in relation to managed research is limited. Institutional research management strategies including setting quality targets and specifying areas of research or types of publication strongly frame the research horizon for academics. In some cases, those strategies include relegating faculty to an inferior academic role, where the sole focus is teaching and service – with lasting consequences on their careers (Lucas, 2004, 2006).

Economy-relevant applied research plays a significant part in universities' research strategies. Locke and Bennion (2010b) showed that, in the UK, academics are more engaged in applied research than in basic research. Recent 'excellence' initiatives in mainland Europe encouraging collaborations between universities engaged in economy-relevant research, such as research networks of 'Réseaux Thématiques de Recherche Avancée' in France, or the 'Exzellenzinitiative' in Germany (Musselin, 2009; Hartwig, 2010), also illustrate this trend. The model of 'competitive clusters', which is being adopted across Europe (Bidan and Dherment, 2009) – based on the Silicon Valley model – encourages transdisciplinary application and collaboration. In the science, economic and socio-economic fields, today's research teams often include top university researchers, private sponsors, small or medium-size enterprises, private researchers, local councils and local or community associations. Research groups and clusters work within specific state-sponsored strategic plans that intricately link science, economy and social issues, and an array of stakeholders. At present, research in the humanities relies on more individual endeavour, although, of late, funding councils such as the Arts and Humanities Research Council in the UK are also starting to favour collaborative work that is applied and economically relevant.

Although cluster research models have been perceived as a 'fad' by some (Martin and Sunley, 2003: 6), on the whole, the socio-economic theory underpinning them has been presented as appealing to both the academy and policy makers for its apparently democratic – 'decentralized' and 'socially progressive' (Martin and Sunley, 2003: 29) – appeal. This model of research is contested from different quarters. Callon and colleagues (2001) in particular, mentioned earlier, have argued for a kind of research that captures the voice of ordinary citizens and problematizes the locus of expertise. They propose that ordinary citizens' involvement in the formulation of research problems, their contribution – not simply as patients or objects of research – to the research process and their participation in and contestation of official dissemination channels all contribute to enriching and democratizing research. The citizen engagement model advocated by Callon and colleagues in which scientists and layperson share knowledge and agree on how a research programme should be oriented has significant implications for research stakes in a globalized world, and for the way research is carried out. It proposes to establish research forums in which actors are 'attached and cluttered' (Callon *et al.*, 2001: 264), rather than detached and stripped of their bodies and identities. Latour's (2010) promotion of a greater critical engagement with research agendas is a related approach. From a socio-cultural perspective, Appadurai brings views that also challenge socio-economic research models; he calls into question the supremacy of what he calls western epistemologies that privilege objectivity at the expense of moral and political considerations (Appadurai, 2000: 14–15). Although I believe the term 'western' needs qualifying, as it demarcates the world too sharply (and those issues are discussed in Chapter 6), I suggest that the perspectives outlined above promote openness, transparency and dialogic engagement with the public and the world, all of which are resonant with the alternative forms of research I examine later in this chapter.

The experience of academics

In previous chapters I have shown how academics can negotiate their own positioning towards the structural constraints of practice by giving a specific inflection to their actions and approaches in practice. When it comes to managed research, however, because of the strong structural determinant in this aspect of the academic role, it is difficult to identify agentic positionings. Although ideological beliefs affecting academics' disciplinary stance might impact on their research orientations, choice is heavily constricted by policy and funding mechanisms. I suggest that the new forms of less managed research, of the type Scott (2009) is envisaging, provide a more accommodative space. Although the dominant mode of research management significantly determines access to or exclusion from what is generally understood as research in the academy, some academics (such as Bernard in the vignette at the beginning of this chapter) can draw on structural resources for their own positioning. In practice, the tensions resulting from competing institutional agendas in respect of research and teaching cannot always be resolved, as illustrated in the words of this academic I interviewed in a UK research-oriented institution:

> Inordinately heavy demands are made both on the quality of teaching and on the quality of research. And inevitably the pressures are to do sort of very high tech research led by research grants, not the sort of thing and not by people who are going to be transferring that knowledge to the students very easily. It's pushing [teaching and research] apart rather than together. That's very unfortunate; it is not a healthy response. Many universities and even this university in some parts have tried to sort of pre-empt the research assessment and say some people are research active and others are not, and those who are not are sort of given piles of teaching and then ignored on the research side.

There is little latitude for academics to find their way into managed research frameworks if they are not targeted and labelled as research active. In teaching-oriented universities, where research may involve requiring some staff to obtain a doctorate, as was the case of the young academic below, support is generally minimal, and research time needs to be accommodated into a heavy workload:

> [The university] will support individuals doing their PhD to the extent that it will pay their fee but – that is what supports the idea that teaching is the most important – they will not give remitted teaching time. So you do your PhD, but we squeeze five days teaching into four, so you've got one day a week when you don't have to be in the university to follow your PhD but you don't get time freed to do that.

Promotion structures, in spite of overt attempts at introducing teaching performance in tenure, in practice remain focused on research performance:

> In this department, teaching is . . . seen as low, demeaning and it is a pain to have to do and you have to get it out the way.
> (Academic in a UK research-intensive institution)

> If you put time and thought into teaching, you are slightly crazy, you are never going to get to the top if you do that because people who do get to

the top put a minimal amount of time into that and they find ways out of it. So they are very very careful with their time.

(Academic in a UK research-intensive institution)

In the same way, and perhaps ironically given the low status attributed to teaching, those who might choose to engage with teaching can be equally constrained in an environment where research outputs matter most:

> It actually took me quite a while to get to teach because, we're mainly research-based here and my boss is really really research-based and he was not very happy for me to teach . . . . One of the conditions of my lectureship was teaching of course, but he sort of hid me away for a year and I had an appraisal and I had not done any teaching and I was worried about it so I went myself and booked myself on the course [for early career academics], and got into teaching that way. And he was a bit 'oh, you are not doing too much teaching are you?' . . . But I would not be able to get a promotion in this department, because my boss actually said to me, 'if you do too much teaching, we might need to look at your contract, you might have to go elsewhere.'

Although it has been suggested (Tapper, 2007: 169) that academics show less aversion from the management of research quality than they do from the management of teaching quality, it has a significant impact on academics' identities, and on the way they locate themselves on the research horizon and strategize their own research development (Lucas, 2006). Where structures point to teaching priorities, it is very difficult – although not impossible – for academics to focus on research. This indirectly relates to Brew and Boud's (2009: 196) finding in a study of over 1,000 Australian academics in research-intensive institutions that there is a relationship between what academics prioritize and their research productivity. Conversely, several of the academics I have spoken to indicated that they needed to strategize and limit the amount of energy spent on teaching, aware of the critical role of research in determining their value on the market, and their professional future, although Brew and Boud (2009) have also proposed that 'absenting' oneself from research was possible through de-prioritizing certain research activities and research development. So, although a degree of agency is possible, I suggest that, on the whole, it is difficult – although not impossible – to prioritize research when an institution's main focus is on teaching. I examine now ways in which it is possible to envisage alternative forms of research.

Towards alternative models of research

The insights into new possibilities for research, conveyed by researchers and philosophers cited earlier who seek to envisage more humanizing and democratic futures for research, contribute to my reflection on models that might offer alternatives to the managed research modes examined so far. They direct the focus on the process of research, rather than on the output. The type of research I examine in this section opens up potentialities for humanizing the research field by questioning the model of objective (value-free) research, allowing multiple methodologies and theoretical perspectives, and new modes of dissemination; and for democratizing through the contribution as partners of non-experts. In exploring these potentialities, I remain mindful of the importance of knowledge legitimization through evidence, critique and publication as accumulative public intellectual capital, and of the need to acknowledge boundaries between knowledge territories, which I discussed earlier in this book.

Focusing on research as a process, I turn to an examination of scholarship on higher education practice – which I see as an example of a potentially sophisticated response to managed research modes. I focus on this form of research as it offers a model whilst being aware that only a minority of academics are today engaged with this kind of research. The term used to describe this type of research signals a form of enquiry that is related to what is known as the Scholarship of Teaching and Learning (SoTL), based on Ernest Boyer's (1990: 17–25) work. Boyer's framework – which tends to be associated with North American practice – identified four types of scholarship (discovery, integration, application and teaching), in which *discovery* refers to discipline-based research – what would normally be understood as research by academics; *integration* represents a form of enquiry that promotes new ways of understanding by integrating into larger intellectual patterns (e.g. through interdisciplinary work); *application* refers to the interface with public and industry or practice-related issues (applied research); and *teaching* refers to the examination of teaching to stimulate active learning and develop creative and critical learners. This framework itself is internally contested, and the field is inhabited equally by researchers using quantitative analyses and by those working in constructivist or relativist research paradigms. I wish to extract, however, what I am examining here from Boyer's framework, which, as Cousin (2008) has incisively noted, points to an implicit hierarchy in which scholarships of discovery and integration are seen as high-status forms of activity, whereas application and teaching scholarships are associated with lower-status forms of enquiry.

To draw out what distinguishes scholarship on higher education practice from dominant research paradigms, I establish its main characteristics with reference to the managed field of higher education research. My analysis is based on Malcolm Tight's (2003) meta-analysis of the main trends in higher education research, which examined higher education research publications and identified three main organizational principles: themes and issues; level of analysis (from a focus on individual student or academic to a focus on the system level); and methods and methodologies. The *themes* identified by

Tight as predominant in higher education research – teaching and learning, course design, the student experience, quality, system policy, institutional management, academic work, knowledge (Tight, 2003: 7) – overlap to a considerable extent with those in scholarship on higher education practice, although those bearing on structural issues may be less prevalent in the latter. The *level of analysis* in scholarship on higher education practice is the micro level in which the researcher is also a practitioner. The *methods/methodologies* for educational research identified by Tight (2003: 8–9) – documentary analysis, comparative analysis, interviews, survey and multivariate analyses, conceptual analysis, phenomenography, critical/feminist perspectives, auto/biographical and observational studies including accounts of personal experience – could all apply to scholarship on higher education practice, which can also include course documentation, cross-campus discussions, documented classroom discussions, curriculum and material development that result in publications, conference presentations or web activities, workshops and reflections on contribution to national and international panels, and collaborations and projects (Huber, 2004: 8). The methods/methodologies used in scholarship on higher education practice are therefore as varied as those used in higher education research, although the documents analysed, the constituencies examined and the observations made are different. The innovative transfer of methods from disciplines to the study of teaching and learning has also been observed (Hutchings and Huber, 2008).

An important element in focusing on research as process is the role of *theory*, which Tight did not examine specifically. There are two aspects to this: (1) the nature of the theorization and (2) the degree of theorization. To address the first point first, theories informing educational research are many and varied. They can relate to learning, teaching, cultures and organizations, sociology of education, knowledge and function of knowledge, or the philosophy of education. All of these subfields are themselves theoretically rich. For most academics, however, scholarship on higher education practice is a secondary domain of enquiry – their main field being in their discipline. Increasingly, academics investigating their practice have brought their own disciplinary theoretical paradigms. From a SoTL perspective, Hutchings (2007) and Hutchings and Huber (2008) have identified, in particular, semiotics (the meaning of images and signs), reader-response theory (linguistics), hermeneutics (linguistics, literature), error and misconceptions (linguistics, language) and resilience (psychology). There is increasing variety and richness in the theories used in SoTL and one can safely conclude that theorizing is available within the process of enquiring on one's practice. The question remains unanswered, however, whether the multiplication of theories necessarily contributes to raising this body of research to the level of the dominant paradigm of higher education research. I suggest that it contributes to destabilizing it as the only paradigm as these multiple theoretical perspectives raise questions about what constitutes knowledge, whether generalization has to be confined to the quantitative paradigm and whether researcher reflexivity is a more reliable means of securing trustworthiness than are positivist approaches. In the same way as Appadurai (2000: 14) suggests that listening to non-dominant models might enrich the dominant western paradigm, I propose that importing from other disciplines into scholarship on higher education practice contributes to enriching understandings of the field of higher education research – itself highly fragmented.

Turning now to the degree to which theory is used in scholarship on higher education practice, anyone who has attended a teaching and learning conference will agree that there is a tremendous degree of variation. Hutchings and Huber (2008), however, question whether it is necessarily useful to oppose theoretical and non-theoretical approaches, claiming that theory building can result from reflection on practical interventions in one's teaching. Brew (2009: 476) cautiously made the suggestion that the new forms of research emerging in higher education constitute a 'complex array of theoretical alternatives to neoliberalism'. Other researchers (Roxå et al., 2008) suggest that SoTL could become a theory-rich field through the input of academic developers. In a suggestion that mirrors Appadurai's (2000: 17) view that the academy has a significant role to play in educating local non-state actors about research stakes so that they can work effectively to respond to global problems, issues and policies, I propose that building bridges between experts and non-experts (which does not mean the end of theory) has worthwhile implications for research and for pedagogies in higher education, which are as yet relatively unexplored. Significantly, fostering undergraduate research and the engagement of students in scholarship on higher education practice (Healey and Jenkins, 2009; Neary and Winn, 2009) also brings in democratizing potential.

Questions about theorizing lead to interrogations regarding the *scope of research claims*. Scholarship on higher education practice is a form of enquiry that is highly situated; its findings cannot be generalized in the sense of being applicable across other contexts. Focusing on the local, however, should not be perceived as a minor endeavour; local evocations are meaningful to other enquirers, and contribute to what is referred to in SoTL as 'the Commons' – a space for knowledge sharing. The need to move away from the dominance of discovery-based epistemological paradigms to promote local investigations that inform the field in different ways and allow for 'naturalistic generalization' (Cousin, 2009: 96) – where the reader is left to draw conclusions with reference to her own field of practice – is useful in informing new ways of thinking about research. The emphasis on the value of local investigations echoes Nussbaum's (2000) proposition that the universal can be reached only through a collection of 'singulars', and that any attempt at analytic generalizing or universalizing is necessarily simplistic.

In respect of the generalizing leverage of theorizing, briefly, one could state that, although theorizing may be perceived as a way of moving from the parochial to the general, one should resist the temptation to 'scientize' applied subjects (Griffiths, 2004: 716). Theorizing can induce the real danger of reducing a field to a range of competing theories that do not talk to each other. Scholarship on higher education practice, I suggest, combining Nussbaum and Latour's terminology, contributes to the making of the rich mosaic of 'singulars' that 'compose' new understandings. New understandings emerge from small-scale findings that have been evidenced through exposure to the real world, the involvement of users in the research process, and dialogic exposure to public contradiction.

I turn finally to the very important issue of *dissemination*. Tight's analysis of managed research in higher education focused exclusively on commercially established peer-reviewed/indexed publications, and did not discuss research that might be published in less well-established outlets, web-based publications or resulting from conference presentations, small projects or enquiry into teaching sponsored by institutions, where the type of scholarship I am describing here is most frequently published. Dissemination of scholarship on higher education practice is, however, an area of striking departure from managed research. Most academics engaged in scholarship on higher education practice disseminate their findings within their own institutions, amongst colleagues, online, in social networks, at summer schools and in teaching and learning conferences. The emphasis is on making their research public, not on competition. The issue of going public is at the heart of the notion of scholarship on higher education practice (Hutchings and Shulman, 1999; Healey, 2000; Huber, 2004; Kreber, 2005).

In sum, as an alternative form of enquiry, scholarship on higher education practice operates in a space where practices and enquiry about practices are critiqued and peer reviewed, and the knowledge generated is at the same time generic, cross-disciplinary and discipline-bound. This space has been called by Huber and Morreale (2002: 2) a 'trading' zone where people exchange ideas as peers. I suggest that the dialogic dynamic created by the specific approach to going public extends that trading zone into a space where research is valued as a process of enquiry advancing the knowledge base through dialogue. This model can inspire alternative forms of research that are open to different epistemologies whilst remaining susceptible of legitimization through critique and peer scrutiny.

Conclusion

In this chapter I have examined some problematic aspects of being a researcher in the academy today. I observed that research came under different guises that do not all have equal status. In respect of managed research, the terrain is particularly subject to structural constraints, and within it it is difficult for academics to devise agentic responses – their engagement in research being heavily framed by the context in which they operate. I have proposed, however, adopting Scott's suggestion that 'counter-forces' have emerged from within the academy (Scott, 2009: xv), that it is possible to develop alternative models to managed research. Using the specific case of scholarship on higher education practice, I suggested that these models offer alternative ways of thinking about research – emulating new epistemological frameworks, alternative patterns of dissemination and a focus on research as process.

In conclusion, I propose that these alternative research models inherently carry a set of double-edged possibilities – the pitfall of careless under-theorized examinations of practice and the risk of multiple methodologies and theoretical frameworks diffusing the impact of knowledge creation as they do not accrete to form a coherent whole. Equally these alternatives hold humanizing and democratizing potential as knowledge is produced by experts who engage with non-experts, and their findings are based on evidence, and offered to contestation through public (including experts and non-experts) arenas of debate. Much remains to be done to promote more broadly democratic research processes that debunk the inadequacy of the discovery/non-discovery dichotomy, and allow for the display and defence of differences in the public space (Callon et al., 2001). One final conundrum remains – is it possible to take on board the humanizing and democratizing dimensions in research, rather than ignoring them in the name of objectivity and value-free knowledge, and to open up the research space to non-experts and non-paradigmatic approaches without severing the thread of commonality woven over generations on which future knowledge wealth is dependent?

Chapter 6

Academic globalism and worldly becoming

Introduction

Because of the complexities it carries, and the multiple perspectives it allows, globalization is a 'thoroughly contested subject' (Rizvi, 2007: 23). This chapter does not propose to go into the details of these conceptual intricacies, although it starts with an outline of its own theoretical position to tackle this complex topic. I focus specifically in this chapter on academics' lived experience of globalization (what I call academic globalism), and examine the tensions they experience in their relation to the global question. In the final section of this chapter, I reflect on the possibility of a role for the academy in shaping a global future that I describe as worldly becoming. This notion is based on Arendt's concept of 'worldliness' and the 'worldly' experience of human beings sharing a 'common world'(Arendt, 1958: 11, 57, 253). I discuss this with reference to a specific educational experience that exemplifies how worldly pedagogies can facilitate understandings of complex global issues. I start with a caution statement in respect of the terminology used in this chapter. I use the terms 'the West' and 'the North' with a strong sense of the reductionism those terms imply, and with a note of caution towards the intellectual inadequacy associated with stereotyping and inflating differences alongside such sharp dichotomies.

The moment of academic practice examined here is complex ('super-complex' even, to bring Barnett back into the discussion); it engages with economic and political notions that are difficult to unravel, and bears on ethically and conceptually intricate issues in terms of the cultural and intellectual questions that it raises. In this discussion there are no simple answers, and no comfortable positions to be talking from, hence, perhaps, a sense for the reader of being drawn into a labyrinth of questions, without being provided with Ariadne's thread to find her way out. My key intention in this chapter is to examine the tensions, as experienced by academics, between economic, intellectual, ethical and ideological stakes in the global question, and to outline the possibility of an academic engagement with worldly becoming. The task is therefore quite bounded in a field that of itself is quite boundless. I start by examining these boundaries (the main questions for higher education), and the main theorizing frameworks from which my own position emerges. In the process, the notions embedded in the title of this chapter are unwrapped.

Global stakes for the academy

Globalization of higher education has generated tensions for academics that include feelings of uncertainty or unease about the meaning of the educational enterprise; ensnarement into complex and contradictory fluxes of raw information; exposure to the interdependencies, interconnections and overlaps of opportunities, practices and ideas; erosion of the time–space dimensions; and immediate replicability, and rapid obsolescence, of products and ideas. Important moral, practical, cognitive and epistemic dilemmas arise from this encounter with global stakes. Universities themselves are operating within flows and turbulences that shape them in ways that they appear unable to predict or influence. Barnett's (2000: 134) metaphor of the university as a 'mosaic on the move' is very powerful to convey this sense of a fluid enmeshment of activities, practices, influences and traffic. The issues that arise from globalization for higher education are not simple or detached. They overlap and resonate with each other to challenge the role of academics, the function of universities and the purpose of higher education. They lead to interrogations in respect of the scope available to academics and to universities both as individual entities and as representatives of some kind of intellectual critique in a field that appears to be firmly in the grip of economic preoccupations. The deepening of the financial crisis as we enter the second decade of this century has only exacerbated the anguish about survival and the tensions between economic, intellectual, ethical and ideological stakes in higher education.

This state of turbulence generates some questioning. The emphasis on competition, industry relevance, measurement of performance and outcome-based education does not always sit comfortably with some of the values and ideologies that academics bring to their practice, which I have discussed throughout this book. Questions arise for the academy. Is the neoliberal agenda here to stay? Should it and can it be resisted? Are the apparent democratizing trends resulting from globalization (staff and student mobility, easier access to information and global knowledge) capable of addressing the disequilibrium and inequalities between those who seem to have some bargaining power in the globalization enterprise, and those who are 'being globalized' (Andreotti, 2008: 56)? What of individuals within the global flows – students, administrators, managers and academics? To quote Ronald Barnett (2005: 3) again, 'Do the actors in those spaces feel that the spaces are theirs to a certain extent?'; is there a sense of 'belongingess' (Nixon, 2011)? Are all academics and all forms of knowledge equal in the global landscape? Are we witnessing the advent of some Orwellian-type of neo-universalism in which university curricula are increasingly similar the world over, and where universality is mainly defined from some hegemonic (neocolonial) western perspective? These questions inform my reflections in this chapter, more as problematics to explore the position of the academy than as hypotheses amenable to validation and statements for action. I suggest, however, that, through contributing to what I have called worldly becoming, the academic endeavour can purposively shape a future that is necessarily global, in which plurality is maintained through approaches that empower both academics and their students.

Theorizing globalization

Of the multiple and contested perspectives on globalization, the focus on the tension between its 'hard' socio-economic dimensions (market liberalization in a neoliberal world, regulation, competition, inequalities) and its 'soft' intellectual, cultural and philosophical dimensions (exposure to difference, values for a global world, cultural supremacies, cosmopolitanism, human rights) is particularly resonant with academic preoccupations. The contiguity to universities and academics of the socio-economic dimension has been examined throughout this book. Although some may be more comfortable than others with the neoliberal agenda, the ways in which academics teach, research, relate to their students and their academic community and carry out their roles as academics are, of necessity, inscribed within the framework of the neoliberal policies that govern higher education, and the competitivity currently inherent in academic practices. I have shown that, on the whole, positions are complex, and not of one piece. The global dimension is not without its own problematics. In practice, academics and universities can explore those soft dimensions through various strategies – for example developing a cosmopolitan outlook, fostering global citizenship approaches or addressing social justice through specific educational content or approaches. Hard and soft dimensions are of course not entirely separate – the link between economic, intellectual, cultural and philosophical is complex but real. Questionings about the meaning of cultures, diversity, multiculturalism, the place of values in the curriculum or the possibilities opened to humanity in a globalized world can be seen as ways of producing counter-narratives – or 'counter-hegemonic projects' (Delanty, 2001: 116) – to the economic tale in which academic practices are presently anchored. They represent potentialities for the bridging of differences and inequalities, and for addressing complex cultural issues through some kind of cosmopolitan activism. They contribute possibly to a shared construction of new imaginaries (Nixon, 2011) and new forms of 'being' for universities (Barnett, 2011).

There have been many suggestions for conceptualizing globalization including a strong emphasis on attending the interplay between *local* and *global* (Giddens, 1990) and the (disputed) idea that the power has increasingly shifted from nation-states to supra-national agencies (King, 2004). Much of the globalization literature builds on Appadurai's (2005: 27–47) conceptualization of a web of 'flows' and 'scapes', in which *scapes* are the configurations that link people and places together (ethnic groups, techniques and communications, for example), and *flows* (or streams) describe the activity along those 'scapes'. Marginson's (2008: 304) identification of 'lateral' differences (differences in languages, pedagogies, scholarship, cultures, organizational systems) and 'vertical' differences (stratifications, hierarchies, inclusion–exclusion, unequal access to being global) within those cross-border flows is also useful to expose differences and gaps in the techno-economic narrative.

For the purpose of what I am examining here – the responses of the academy to the tensions in the global question – I find the line adopted by a number of authors (Appadurai, 2000; Brecher *et al.*, 2000; Robins and Webster, 2002; Apple *et al.*, 2005) quite useful. It is related to Falk's (1994: 139) characterization of global citizenship in which he distinguishes between 'globalisation from above', which focuses on broad globalizing trends, and 'globalisation from below', which focuses on agentic and local manifestations. This way of theorizing globalization overlaps with the global–local dynamic of Giddens. At the risk of oversimplifying, globalization from above is conceptualized as a structural phenomenon and examined from a techno-economic perspective as an outcome of late capitalism and technologization; globalization from below problematizes the political and human implications of neoliberalism, and focuses on people, minority voices and localisms within the structural trends. This dual framework has its limitations in presenting the two perspectives as entirely distinct and not rendering fully the conceptual complexity (Apple *et al.*, 2005). It also attenuates the notion that globalization is a 'process' (King, 2004: 45) rather than 'a finished and complete world order' (Urry, 2002: 21). I give this distinction a specific slant in this chapter and focus on globalization of higher education from below as the local responses of the academy to the challenges, inequalities and gaps inherent in globalization of higher education from above.

Frequent flyers and global stars

At a basic level, being a global academic is about being connected with colleagues and students across the world. Academics teach and carry out research online, outside the physical place of work. Academic presence has become virtual and ubiquitous, the workspace increasingly ill-defined and work collaborators distributed worldwide. Being global is also simply about taking part in global intellectual gossip networks – knowing who is getting what position; who has left which institution, why and to go where; and generally being informed of the global academic scene in one's field. The connectivity afforded to academics today makes tenuous the frontier between professional and personal dimensions; an academic I spoke to called this informal form of engagement with colleagues across the world 'the blurry area between research, scholarship and friendship'. This is sustained through electronic mail, the use of Skype, social networks and a regular exchange of electronic links that bind and connect groups and individuals.

The intellectual flows created by the 'network society' (Castells, 2010: 22), and the cheap modes of travel available today, play a significant role in enabling virtual and real globalism in the academy. The most familiar example of academic globalism is the international conference. Helena's reflections on this, in the vignette below, will read to many like a well-known scenario.

Vignette seven: Helena as a global academic

As Chair in Health Policy at a South African university, Helena is presently involved in an international research programme involving epidemiologists, sociologists and health policy specialists from Australia, Canada and South Africa on social determinants of health inequality. Her work on perinatal mortality has had a lot of impact outside South Africa, including in India, the United States and South America. She is regularly invited to deliver keynotes on her research, and attends international colloquia and conferences on a regular basis. In the course of an ordinary working day, she spends more time communicating with colleagues across the world than with her own university colleagues, which sometimes feels odd. She also spends quite a lot of time outside the university as this specific project takes her into the field to study populations and also includes numerous meetings with health and government representatives. Helena always looks forward to these large scientific gatherings, which give her and the research team a chance to catch up on the latest advances and latest debates – not to mention the gossip without which she would not feel part of this scientific community. She prepares with a degree of trepidation for the next colloquium, which will be held in Philadelphia.

Quite apart from the obvious intellectual value she draws from these travels, and the feeling of re-uniting with her disciplinary family at each conference, she cannot help but think with a degree of amusement about what she calls the 'peripheries of academic conferences', all the paraphernalia characteristic of any international conference. She thinks especially of the Opening Ceremony and the highly romanticized Gala Dinner. Each offers, almost every time, a chance to revel in some aspects of national culture, even if the meaning of the rituals displayed remains relatively obscure to most delegates. She cannot help but think that the cultural displays witnessed at international conferences have a tokenistic quality to them. They are sometimes right on the verge of caricature. She thinks back to the traditional blessing of the land and the sound of the Ydaki greeting the delegates in Sydney; the opera singer in Prague; and the haggis ceremony in Edinburgh. In her own country she remembers distinctly the Zulu dancing at a conference in Swaziland. She wonders about the relation of those national rituals to the international contexts in which scientists such as her work. Although looking forward to the Philadelphia colloquium in October and the cultural delights this will offer, she wonders about the value and meaning of these connections to local cultural folklore. Who is speaking through these manifestations of local cultures, and what are they saying, to whom? Is it ever perceived as anything other than an amusing but innocuous nod in the direction of the overwhelmingly absent host nation?

The experience of Helena and her slightly ironic take on the global experience of academics abroad is reminiscent – nationalism aside – of Ulrich Beck's (2006: 4) encounter with a 'global' Danish businessman who loved the European Union but preferred to think of himself as a Danish person – itself evocative of Richard Falk's (1994: 134) encounter with a similar Danish traveller evolving in a 'kind of homogenized elite global culture'. Beside the sanitized imagery conveyed by conference folklore, this vignette serves to highlight the first equity issue (gap) about globalization of higher education in this chapter. Although virtual academic globalism (the ability to be global through technology) is available, to some extent, to all, real globalism (travelling) is not. Real globalism provides opportunities for exposure to different cultures and different ways of seeing the world – in theory, at least. In practice, international conferences are often linguistically and culturally bounded, and exposure to difference limited. Academic travels abroad are also often cushioned from exposure to the local cultures.

These introductory comments provide a glimpse into the complexity and diversity of what being a global academic actually entails; at a very basic level, being global is about forming worldwide connections and occupying an intellectual position in the global field. A note on the precariousness of the global enterprise is, however, introduced at this early stage. It is reminiscent of Helena's ironic remarks in the vignette, and draws attention to another important issue in the global narrative – the direction of cultural flow:

Rather than say my experience of higher education is global, I would say it is one of an Anglophone environment. Whenever I go to conferences and build new links, the follow-through is more with colleagues from English-speaking countries – the US, Australia, South Africa. I do make contacts with Europeans, but they tend to fall away, they are not sustained. I experience the world but the links are fragile. And that's for two reasons mainly: (1) we don't produce anything together, we don't write together, (2) sheer lack of time. It is hard enough to keep up with the local community, let alone the global one. And I must say for someone who like me has lived abroad quite a lot, I experience quite a lot of frustration from this, the fragility of the connections that are made. And relation to the location is also fragile. We are all locked out in an international hotel, with very little to do with the local community. It is the same Novotel whether you are in Sydney or in Vancouver. So globalization does not provide access to foreignness, you are cocooned from the world really.

(UK academic)

Flaws in the flow

In the course of my professional activities, and in the discussions informing this book, I have met academics who did not appear to locate their work, their practice or their identity within a global framework. Often those academics who did not see themselves as global were heavily involved in their own local practice (often with heavy teaching loads) with little time to consider connections, even with present colleagues, except for those with whom they were teaching. They appeared to be so overwhelmed by their own struggle to get on with the job, or engaged with the professional aspects of their discipline, that they displayed little inclination to look elsewhere and engage globally. I focus here, however, on those who consider themselves as global academics and whose activities may include working in international collaborative teams, sharing research findings at international conferences, working abroad for periods of time, teaching internationally distributed online programmes, being engaged in academic exchanges and being invited to give specialist seminars abroad. Within this range, again, there are nuances in the local–global work balance. The view expressed by this UK academic, however, sums up that of many in the academy:

> I like to think that I am an international scholar. I have worked with collaborators in China, in Australia, in the States, and in South Africa. You can't be a researcher without linking with the rest of the world.

It is notable that much of the globalizing for academics is anchored (more or less tenuously) in their research. For them, the richness of the process and the quality of the product resulting from international collaborations is obvious. The whole is presented as better than the sum of its parts. In some testimonies, the issue of linguistic or cultural disadvantage is quickly brushed aside. 'Theory is a great globaliser because it gives you a universal language to speak to others with', said one UK academic I spoke to. Some academics, however, address the often unspoken gaps and inequalities within this globalizing bliss. As English is the language of globalization and the chosen language for research, West/North-inspired worldviews are privileged: 'The literature we read is global; they are westernized papers because it is in English, but still they are international' (UK academic).

The supremacy of English as the language of research dissemination is, however, problematic. Even if it does not coerce into westernizing, it excludes many and therefore limits exposure to difference. Economic factors are limitative too; some academics are able to be more global than others, depending on the context in which they work, the subject they research and their disciplines/fields. It was suggested that pure research is easier to transfer to the global than more professionally oriented (and culturally dependent) subjects.

Flaws in the bliss go far beyond the well-rehearsed issue of linguistic hegemony. The question of North/West supremacy and of the unevenness in the flow of traffic was raised, for example, by a French-speaking Canadian academic who works regularly with collaborative partners in Europe, North Africa and South America:

> In my relations with European networks, we focus on research, so we speak within the same frames of reference, we speak in the same logic – which is very western in nature – we have read the same books, possibly attended the same universities, so we share cultural and conceptual points of reference. In my relation with the South, it is more about development, aid, sharing of my expertise, and up until now there hasn't been the same connection as with Europe, although I feel that this might develop into collaborations, at the moment, you can't call these collaborations. (My translation)

He suggested that there is a form of complicity on the part of his partners in Africa, especially in fostering a kind of post-colonial relationship:

> In those North–South relations, they also see us, because we come from North America, they see us as if we ought to know more and better than them. This notion of relying on a European or a North American academic to learn the truth about something brings about a fraught type of relationship; we are not talking as equals, and after a while, I feel uncomfortable with that! I need more reciprocal exchanges, so I am working on this. In North Africa, especially, I don't see it evolving into any kind of reciprocal egalitarian collaboration, not because I don't wish it to happen, but because this is the way they are used to functioning, especially with Europe. It would really take a lot of shaking up to work collaboratively on an equal footing. (My translation)

Outside research collaborations, the issue of inequality in educational markets has been well rehearsed in the context of internationalization (Naidoo, 2005; Altbach and Knight, 2007; Altbach and McGill Peterson, 2008). As another example of the gaps between academic aspirations and the economic agenda – the mercantile dimension of the internationalizing agenda – it is presented as conflicting starkly with academic endeavour in the views of this Australian academic I spoke to:

The university was driving for money and students. It was all money-driven. As teachers it had a huge impact that has gone off the radar. We were pushed very hard to internationalize. We started to look towards Asia. The whole view was Asia, Asia, Asia!

There is no scope within this chapter to fully explore this significant issue of internationalization, and I shall simply highlight here instances of the ideological tensions this agenda can generate. Some clearly find their engagement with international students fulfilling, as is the case below for this UK research professor:

> Some of my best teaching moments have been with postgraduate students in Beijing – when you can get them doing, it's fantastic. The level of intellectual engagement is almost awe-inspiring.

However, significant ideological tensions were expressed by the Australian academic cited earlier, which underscore the potential for clashing with academic values discussed throughout this book:

> In the faculty where I was working, almost all the students were Chinese – Chinese, Vietnamese or from Hong Kong. Their agenda was rather different from ours. It was not a positive cultural exchange, there was a lot of stereotyping. They were paying a lot of money and they came wanting – and of course this is a massive generalization – they came wanting a piece of paper and in some cases, one that they would get at all cost. It really challenged us – having to think of them as clients. Thinking about how far do we change to accommodate them, and how far we say 'no this is what higher education is about and that's what we value, and what we think higher education is about' – even if they are paying for it. It caused an enormous degree of angst. This was a challenge to thinking that HE is about being critical, being challenged, being autonomous, having to sink or swim – I guess those are quite old-fashioned ideas of education. And some might say maybe that's a narrow western view, and we should perhaps hold their hands.

The conflict with what I have called earlier *reproduction* ideologies cannot be underestimated. If academics cannot reproduce or take forward the values they believe in, the relation to international students becomes difficult – fraught even. It engenders beliefs about international students' approaches and motivations, and attitudes towards language ability that feed into mainstream academic practices:

> Doing research with foreign students is difficult, they have problems with English, they have to mix with other students, they don't have the social skills and we end up with late research, with reports that are written by

supervisors, and then research students expect a professional career, or many expecting you to find them an academic position.

(UK academic)

Direction of cultural flow is central to the issues I discuss here. Where cultural differences cannot be explored, let alone bridged, the accusation levelled against globalization of simply being an exercise in westernizing or americanizing the world becomes tangible. The academic endeavour can be either deflected from its purpose or severely compromised through blindness or clumsiness towards the issue of directionality in cultural flows. Conceptions of multiculturalism that suggest a blanket respect of difference and disregard any values, or the weight (or legitimacy) of evidence, are hardly more helpful. They encourage relativism. They reflect an entrapment into what Beck (2006: 12) has called the 'national prison theory of human existence' – that is, deterministic, provenance-driven views of identity. Neither the export of western values to the rest of the world nor naïve multiculturalism can provide a satisfactory answer to the ethical dilemmas academics may find themselves in when the issue of human rights is not openly addressed (Phillips, 2007), as one of the academics I spoke to noted:

At X, I worked a lot with people in Saudi Arabia. To what extent was this about democratizing anything? I would say zero! There were no women, we were educating men who would be educating men, using western knowledge. I guess to some extent we were trying to take into account their paradigm, but some of it we were finding quite offensive to be honest . . . To what extent having an international approach means you have to give up your own beliefs about openness, the right to critique, etc. . . . I guess that's something I have been wrestling with all my life, and I haven't got an answer to it.

Finally, geography and geopolitics also play a part in power-steering cultural flows. In countries outside what is referred to as the North or the West, the pragmatic necessity to work globally is more pertinent, as illustrated by these Australian and South African (English-speaking) voices:

I suppose you can exist in the UK and you don't feel like you're starving. There is a fairly vibrant community of research, and a large number of people, and the smallness of the geography, so you can probably exist without travelling. But for Australians, because we are so far away and the numbers are so small, it is difficult.

(Australian academic)

For academics in emerging economies, working globally can be seen as a way of enhancing one's academic credentials at home:

This [South African] university thinks it is a world-class institution. There is an explicit valuing of academics going overseas and to think of yourself as a global academic. And there is funding to promote working with top institutions across the globe. Thinking about ourselves globally is part of the transformation agenda, compensating for lack of cultural capital – making up, in a sense.

(South African academic)

These policies are perceived as possibly increasing local inequalities within regions where dominant countries favour global partners over closer neighbours:

For most academics in the vast majority of South African universities they are sufficiently well connected in the technical sense, to be able to work collaboratively, especially with partners in the North. Partnerships in the region are much more difficult. Colleagues in Africa are not so well connected, travel in Africa is not easy. That's because of history, logistics, uneven development, etc. If we are serious about our position on the continent, we have to get better than that.

(South African academic manager)

A Namibian academic I spoke to about globalization was quick to bring into the discussion the issue of western responsibility:

Those who promote social and restorative justice today are seconded from Europe. They are the descendants of the same white oppressors who came at the beginning of the nineteenth century. So the West came to the South, brought its nineteenth century ideas, and then left. It left behind those ideas, and the people are still struggling with what they left two-hundred years ago. It is crippling people's thoughts.

To take stock at this stage, globalization from below, as translated in the experience of academics, points to issues concerning equity of access to a globalized academe (and exclusion for some); the tension between the economic agendas of universities, and the intellectual and ideological aspirations of academics; the related questioning of the direction of cultural flow; and local inequalities created through single-handed harnessing of the global agenda by the most privileged universities in the developing world, as in the case of the South African testimony above. These points do not exhaust the issues related to globalization from below; however, they give a sense that the shaping of global worldviews through a North/West lens and the resulting issues of cultural differences are central to the academy's questioning. This narrative is moderated by indications that the North/West could learn from values prevalent in other parts of the world. The desire to learn from rather than be listened to was expressed in many of the conversations, as a form of from-below response to an apparently one-way flow. Authentic engagement with the world works in subtle ways for individuals as they choose to engage as equals, and to listen to the world as much as being listened to. This can translate, for example, into careful approaches to writing:

> All the time, as I am writing, I am conscious that my work is going to be read around the world. I deliberately try to write in such a way that my work will reach out all around the world, in different cultures, in different situations, different kinds of audience. I am very conscious of that and I am trying to communicate with the widest possible audience – which means the world, the globe. So that's part of my being as a global academic. I am concretely situating not just my ideas and my research but my actual writing – the construction of sentences, the formation of phrases. I am doing that with the whole world in my mind. Of course, one can only do that to a certain extent, but that is a guiding principle of mine. It is very firm, very deep within me, and it poses enormous challenges.
>
> (UK academic)

Worldly becoming

In this examination of globalization of higher education from below, I now turn to the question of a possible meaningful cosmopolitan engagement for the academy. This section – although based on a concrete example – represents what I see as a potentiality, or a 'feasible utopia' (Barnett, 2011: 4). Cosmopolitanism has been described as a vision (Beck, 2006), a process (Hill, 2000) and an ethical/moral perspective (Appiah, 2005; Nixon, 2011) on the world. Beyond the important epistemological and ontological considerations it carries, there is a strong 'teleological' (purposeful moral end) dimension to 'cosmopolity' (Nixon, 2011: 52). Cosmopolitanism does not simply establish new ways of understanding the world, but devises actions to transform it. The form of cosmopolitan engagement I describe here may have been embryonic in some of the academics I have met (it is contained in *transformative* ideologies). To the term 'cosmopolitan', however, I prefer 'worldly', as being less connoted with evangelizing virtues than is 'cosmopolitan'. What I mean specifically by worldly becoming is the purposive setting up of strategies through which the potential brought about by globalization can be mobilized to engage in shaping understandings of how to live with uncertainty and supercomplexity in a shared common world, in ways that preserve plurality. My stance is inspired by the work of Hannah Arendt, who associates 'worldliness' with the sharing of a common world that 'transcends our lifespan into past and future alike' (Arendt, 1958: 55). This worldliness is threatened by 'worldlessness', which 'as a political phenomenon is possible only on the assumption that the world will not last' (p. 54).

For Arendt, human endeavour is about the sharing of a common world that can be sustained only through plurality:

> Under the conditions of a common world, reality is not guaranteed primarily by the 'common nature' of all men who constitute it, but rather by the fact that, differences of position and the resulting variety of perspectives notwithstanding, everybody is always concerned with the same object. If the sameness of the object can no longer be discerned, no common nature of men, least of all the unnatural conformism of a mass society, can prevent the destruction of the common world, which is usually preceded by the destruction of the many aspects in which it presents itself to human plurality.
>
> (Arendt, 1958: 58)

The emphasis on a world that is common and shared and can continue to exist only because of the inherent plurality of humans within it is useful. This final section focuses on educational approaches that might (or could) inform a worldly dimension for higher education. Of the 'ecological' university – which he sees as a 'feasible utopia' – Barnett (2011: 144) says it 'reveals itself, in the first place, through its care *for* the world, and not in its impact *on* the world' (p. 144, italics in original). A sense of purposive collective enterprise, shared endeavour, common destiny and a yet-to-be-realized potential is inherent in the idea of worldly becoming.

I suggest in this section ways in which higher education can mediate and exploit the complex issues raised by globalization to promote change. Examining the contribution of the academy to worldly becoming brings back the theme of educational ideologies that runs through this book, and the meaning that academics give to their action in the higher education sphere. I make specific reference to a pedagogical experience that was examined as carrying this kind of educational potential. It is important to indicate, first, that it is not a pedagogic prescription but rather an exploration of pedagogical potentialities and, second, that it is not the only proposition 'on the block'; there are other ways of responding to the challenges that the world's complexity offers, and of developing cosmopolitanism – or purposive contribution to worldly becoming.

In my encounters with academics, I came across those who enacted this worldly becoming dimension in their engagement with students; those who described their disciplines in such ways that their emphasis was on developing global awareness and addressing planetary preoccupations fell into this category too. With nuances, pedagogies of engagement (Barnett and Coate, 2005; Barnett, 2007), capabilities pedagogy (Walker and Nixon, 2004; Walker, 2006; Nixon, 2011), 'responsive' pedagogies (Singh, 2005), critical pedagogy (Apple, 1993; Freire, 1996; Darder, 2002, 2003) and global citizenship (Andreotti, 2006; Bourn *et al.*, 2006; Bourn, 2009) are instantiations of these approaches. These educational approaches present potentialities for the university as a site capable of working towards sustaining a common world – as described by Arendt. I have touched on those forms of pedagogies in Chapter 3, and shall not return to them specifically.

In the last section of this final chapter, I would like to discuss a study that examined an educational initiative which involved Palestinian and Israeli students in a three-year period of study in the UK. Broadly, the study investigated, through interviews with students on this programme, pedagogies that appeared to be suited to enhancing understandings across communities engaged in an ongoing live conflict. The student data cited below were collected for that study (Fanghanel and Cousin, 2011).

This was an extreme educational experience, and extreme examples are not necessarily the most apt at providing directions for mainstream situations. However, they can serve to illustrate a range of possibles, and broaden the horizon of potentialities for thinking about higher education. This specific example is rich enough to inform theoretically an examination of the challenges facing the academy as it allows for an empirical insight into the issue raised earlier regarding the balance to be struck between naïve multiculturalism and the temptation to disseminate western views to the rest of the world. It does this in four ways:

- it was a case study of how to bring together, in an educational space, views rooted in strong and conflicting national and religious histories and identities;
- it provided ways of reflecting on how to shift people's view from one way of seeing the world to multiple ways of seeing it, without emphasizing relativist epistemologies;
- it promoted a non-essentialist theory of identity and 'an affirmation of the other as both different and the same' (Beck, 2006: 58);
- it empowered students with the potential to develop ways of acting and behaving (or 'functioning' in a 'capabilities' framework) differently in the world.

The form of pedagogy used on the programme was described as worldly pedagogy, which was defined as:

[A pedagogy that] seeks to educate towards an understanding of global questions in the context of a common world shared by plural human beings, in which plurality is a condition for the world's sustainability. It is predicated on a desire to empower students through understandings of that plurality outside of the dualistic perspectives of West/non-West apprehensions of culture, and without resorting to relativist theories of knowledge.

(Fanghanel and Cousin, 2011)

Pedagogically, there were two significant characteristics to this educational experience that I wish to discuss here as relevant to education for worldly becoming: first, the theory of knowledge on this programme (a combination of experiential and proposition knowledge); second, its stance on difference (a problematization of difference presented as inherent in national or provenance identities).

In examining the theories of knowledge deployed in this programme, I return to the issue of ideologies in the curriculum discussed in Chapter 3, and draw more specifically on the post-constructivist position discussed earlier in this book. Young (2008) has convincingly argued for re-introducing to the curriculum context-independent knowledge – that is, knowledge that is objective (external to the knower), conceptual and valid beyond the context of production or transmission. Empowering learners with access to 'powerful knowledge' and the intellectual tools to go beyond the experiential, in Young's own words, provides them with the means 'to overcome their oppression' (p. 25). I suggest that it is key to any purposive pedagogic endeavour. The pedagogies used on the programme discussed here were reliant on a balance of context-independent and context-dependent knowledge. The programme entailed a series of lectures on the history and politics in the region, and participants indicated that these help them understand their own stance and develop their own ways of thinking and of articulating arguments about the conflict. Through these they understood their own misapprehensions, the impact of their own national and provenance scripts and of the education they had received, as illustrated by this Palestinian respondent:

> So the fact that I came here, I managed to do many things that I would never have been able to do in Gaza, it opened my eyes on the world. My opinions haven't changed. But I've learnt to listen to the others and sometimes understand their point of view. I added to my own schema, my own opinions, my own understanding, new things I wasn't aware of before. That's what has happened.

There were several testimonies on the value that students put on accessing propositional knowledge, and how they thought that this had contributed to their intellectual maturation. At the same time, through recourse to narrative and context-dependent knowledge (narratives from fellow students, exposure to respective national rituals, common sharing of news from the region, etc.), they learnt to discover a common human dimension in their experience, which destabilized their initial views. One Palestinian student said that this experience had 'rocked [his] world'. An Israeli student explained that he could no longer simply think from an Israeli perspective: 'When I see things, when I hear about things I have lost the ability to think about it only from the Israeli point of view'.

It can be argued that, to be effective, approaches for worldly oriented education must integrate this abstract exposure to facts and concepts, and the rich human experience inherent in sharing a common world. The two types of knowledge played two different functions. Propositional knowledge about the history and politics of the region helped students understand aspects they had never fully known or problematized about their own nation. Experiential knowledge (by bringing them together as human beings) helped them carve a space where reasoned discussions could take place. In this space different voices could be heard, and different values discussed. Access was provided to 'the language of deliberative democracy' (Nixon, 2004: 114). This approach is therefore less about developing one's own sense of self, or finding the connection between the local and the global, than about developing through deliberation an informed judgement that allows to-ing and fro-ing between the local and global. This is an enactment of what is close to Appiah's (2005: 223) notion of 'rooted cosmopolitanism', for whom 'a cosmopolitanism with prospects must reconcile a kind of universalism with the legitimacy of at least some forms of partiality' – what Beck (2006: 60) has called 'contextual universalism'. It is also close to Robins and Webster's (2002) view of a cosmopolitan university, and as indicated earlier Barnett's (2011: 141) conceptualization of the 'ecological university'. In the process of learning about the history and politics of their region, and getting to know each other, concepts of difference were problematized. One Palestinian respondent explained how this helped him understand complexity:

> And if you asked me what about my experience that's definitely changed. If before I might have said that person is crazy about the way he is thinking . . . now I would say that's the way he thinks, it is his right to think that way. There is a lot of grey and very small black and white.

An educational experience that emphasizes commonalities within significant delineations of differences and conceives of plurality as inherent in sustaining a common world – in the Arendtian (1958) vision referred to earlier – provides scope for thinking and imagining otherwise. The potential of any such pedagogy for resisting partisan arguments and fostering understandings of variations as distributed beyond the fault lines of specific religious or national groupings is considerable.

Conclusion

In this chapter I have examined some of the issues facing the academy in a globalized world. Having adopted a theorizing line that disentangles structural (from above) from agentic (from below) representations, I focused specifically on the second aspect to begin to unknot the tensions identified in academics' narratives in respect of globalization. Within this, I explored academic globalism as an empirical lived state of being in a global world, and worldly becoming as a meaningful potentiality for an engagement of the academy with this global world. In the instantiations of academic globalism emerging from academics' narratives, I identified tensions in respect of unequal access (absence of some academics from real globalism); linguistic disequilibrium as research (and increasingly teaching) is conducted in English; and direction of cultural flow as linguistic supremacy inevitably leads to cultural supremacy and as mercantile intentions appear to dominate the internationalizing agenda. An important question posed by academics in this context was that of the North/West direction of traffic in global exchanges, and of the inherent dangers in not resisting both westernization inspired by some kind of neocolonial endeavour, and unproblematized multiculturalism. In the final section of this chapter, I provided the baseline for a possible framework for worldly education that entails a complex theory of knowledge, and careful theorizing of identity and difference.

In conclusion, I offer some tentative answers to the questions raised at the beginning of the chapter. Mercantilism and performativity are threatening to shift the academic endeavour away from humanistic and intellectual considerations, and this needs to be counter-balanced. The related risk of an Orwellian type of neo-universalism generating assimilation and uniformity is equally tangible. A sophisticated and robust critique of these drifts, a clear articulation of strategies for engaging with worldly becoming, and adherence to knowledge frameworks that empower learners are needed to counter them. The positioning of some academics towards this threat, as discussed throughout this book, exemplifies that counter-inflection; it is difficult to see whether it is powerful enough, and sustainable in the present climate. Seeking to favour approaches that steer away from westernizing neocolonialism without uncritically embracing multiculturalism requires careful treading. It necessitates the purposeful development of approaches that can harness the difficult cultural, political and value agendas whilst relying on robust theories of knowledge that empower both students and the academy. The positions outlined here as contributing to worldly becoming point to a role for universities as safe sites for intellectual critique, and for the academy as a major contributor to the shaping of a common shared global future.

Conclusion

Being an academic

As I reach the final part of this study, I summarize the main points of an analysis that broadly has led me to consider the academy's various forms of responses to the neoliberal agenda underpinning academic practices in today's universities. Building on responses that offer potentialities for a form of academic engagement that centres on the relation of education to society and the world, and based on suggestions I have made throughout this book towards outlining the shape of this engagement, I then sketch out what I see as a possible contribution of the academy to addressing complexity and uncertainty in a global world.

This book set out to examine what being an academic in today's universities meant. I have explored different facets of academic life through academics' own narratives, and with reference to the cultures and regimes within which they operate, and the frameworks that structure their practice. The main aim of this book was to examine the lived experience of academics in practice, as distinct from espoused depictions that might circulate because they are part of academic folklore or because of the way they appear to emerge from policies and regimes inherent in the work context. In the process of this analysis, focusing on the agentic responses of academics in practice, I highlighted the empowering potential residing within the academy to counter-balance the neoliberal stance that pervades higher education.

The underpinning theoretical stance adopted in this book emerged from my own reflections in previous work on the complex interplay between agency and structure, and more specifically the multi-dimensionality of agency, and the richness and materiality of the interaction of agents with structures. The focus of this journey was on the ideologies that inhabit the actions and aspirations of academics and colour their understandings and approaches to their role. I organized this exploration around three main ideological orientations. *Production* ideologies refer to education in its relation to the production of human capital with an emphasis on the direct link between higher education and the world of work. *Reproduction* ideologies convey conceptions of the value of education for its own sake, and emphasize transmitting and advancing disciplinary knowledge to reproduce the next generation of discipline experts. *Transformation* ideologies envisage education as a means towards social, personal, human or global transformation. I have shown that these ideologies circulate throughout the educational engagement of academics in different forms, and at different levels of practice. They represent different conceptions of education and different values framing the academic endeavour. I have shown that these ideologies are not of one piece, or entirely bounded, and that they can co-exist within an individual academic. From within this overarching framework, I have explored six moments of practice.

The first moment focused on the responses of academics to the policies in place in universities to manage practice and performance and broadly labelled 'managerialism' and the related management technology underpinning it, which Lyotard (1984) has called 'performativity'. Following on from Deem and her colleagues' (2007: 27) suggestion that managerialism is 'routinely resisted, avoided and adapted', I examined the way academics positioned themselves towards the policies framing their practice. Academics' positioning is informed by their own histories, trajectories and ideologies, which provide material to adopt, adapt or resist in different ways. I have established that academics' positioning was not of one piece; their responses often included a mix of adoption and resistance. I have shown, for example – with some cautionary reservations – that some academics were able to appropriate the neoliberal agenda, and adapt it to suit their own transformative educational aspirations. This theme of the empowering potential residing within the academy as they enact their own stance is central to this book, and was developed in further chapters.

The second moment of practice focused on early career academics, and the programmes that have emerged, in the UK, Australia and New Zealand in particular, to support early career academics' teaching development. I discussed the context in which those programmes emerged in the UK and the controversies surrounding their introduction. I examined, with reference to formal evaluations and my own data on this topic, the impact of these programmes on academics. Some significant benefits were identified, which included exposure to different disciplinary perspectives, and to institutional structures, and the potential for self-actualization that could be derived from exposure to the body of research on teaching and learning. I also highlighted three areas that were particularly problematic in respect of the impact of these programmes on early career academics. First, they do not fully harness the issue of transfer to the context of practice, which is not automatic or unproblematic (e.g. Guile and Young, 2003; Tuomi-Gröhn and Engeström, 2003). Second, they underestimate the obstacles that programme participants will encounter in respect of local policy, hierarchies and practices that might contradict or hinder enactment of what they have been taught on these courses. Finally, these courses may convey values that are incongruent with participants' own educational ideologies, and this necessarily limits the learning impact of these courses. I suggested that more empowering models for reflecting on teaching and learning needed to be developed that would not reinforce hierarchies within the academy, but rather contribute to promoting dialogic learning environments, citing scholarship on higher education practice as an example of such models.

Chapter 3 focused on conceptions of the student and learning in the academy. I examined conceptions that presented the student as 'consumer' as a dominant model in the academy, particularly in the UK, where the emphasis on student choice and student satisfaction is stressed, and engineered through policy, and the relation to the economy is proactively encouraged in the curriculum. Having established that there were a number of possible conceptions available to qualify the relation of academics to students I examined another four separate conceptions. The student 'as becoming' and the student 'as vehicle for social transformation' were identified as respectively conveying reproduction and transformation ideologies of education. I suggested that these, as sophisticated responses to the 'consumer' and 'deficiency' conceptions, might provide a solid basis for a questioning of the present educational orthodoxy and for a re-imagining of the relation between students and academics, especially as it is underpinned by conceptions of the student as 'recipient of the desire to teach'.

The fourth moment of practice was the discipline. This chapter examined the discipline as a distinctive feature of higher education, a strong locus for academic identity and a defining structure for universities' organization. The emphasis was on establishing this moment of practice as contested from outside the academy, and open to ideological interpretations from within. The status of the discipline in today's universities has come under attack as university learning and research have opened to the external world and engaged in issues of a societal or generic nature, beyond the discipline. From within, I examined instantiations of the discipline in practice, and academics' own interpretations of their discipline. I highlighted nuances and overlaps in the three main ideological orientations of production, reproduction and transformation. I concluded that disciplines were more than abstract epistemological constructs or structural entities. I have suggested that the analytical focus on the micro level of practice provides heterogeneous views of academic identities and represents the discipline as a lively entity that is significantly influenced by the external world and the way academics relate to it. In that sense, it contributes to the re-imagining of academic identities called for by Barnett and Di Napoli (2008).

Chapter 5 focused on research and argued that universities are increasingly accommodating diverse modes of research. This multimodality was examined through an explanatory framework that included socio-historical, epistemological, management and policy-driven components. Managed research was described as an area of practice where it was difficult for academics to position themselves freely. Alternative modes of research – and the specific example of scholarship on higher education practice – were discussed as capable of serving as counter-models and carrying the potential to infuse new energy. I discussed specifically issues about researcher objectivity, relation to non-experts, theorizing, and generalization of findings. I suggested that scholarship on higher education practice could serve as an inspirational model to develop a more open, humanized and democratic research space.

Chapter 6 focused on the academic in a global world and the responses of the academy to the global question. It explored academic globalism as an empirical lived state of being for an educator and researcher in a global world, and worldly becoming as a form of engagement through which the potential brought about by globalization could be mobilized to shape understandings of how to live with uncertainty and supercomplexity in a shared common world, in ways that preserve plurality. From the perspective of the experience of academics, tensions were identified that related to unequal access to globalism; linguistic imbalance as research (and increasingly teaching) is conducted in English; direction of cultural flow; and the issue of local inequalities within specific contexts. A troublesome issue raised by academics was that of the North/West direction of traffic in global exchanges. I discussed the necessity to move away from visions that equate to disseminating western views to the rest of the world as much as from those that foster naïve multiculturalism without problematizing difference. In the final section of this chapter, the focus was on worldly becoming. With reference to an educational initiative that encouraged students to work within and beyond conflict, and in relation to approaches discussed in Chapter 3, I provided an illustration of the type of curricula that might contribute to worldly becoming. This included a theory of knowledge integrating propositional and experiential learning, and careful theorizing of identity and difference emphasizing commonalities within significant delineations of differences. I concluded that the threat of shifting the academic endeavour away from humanistic and intellectual considerations was real and that a sophisticated and robust critique of these drifts, a clear articulation of strategies for harnessing worldly becoming and adherence to knowledge frameworks that empower academics and learners were needed to counter them. This pointed to a role for universities as safe sites of intellectual critique, and for the academy as a major contributor to shaping the global future.

The stakes are high to successfully take the academy through what seems a labyrinthine future. The tensions identified in the six moments of practice examined in this book have highlighted the impact of the neoliberal agenda on academic practices, and both the threats for the academy, and the potential for resisting and transforming this agenda. As a number of authors have shown (Musselin, Scott, King, Barnett and Delanty *inter alia*), as one looks at universities over time, change rather than stasis comes across as a key feature of the academic landscape. Or, rather, one witnesses a balance between change and stability, with the endurance of values deeply anchored in the academic psyche counter-balancing policies and trends that might threaten the intellectual and ethical principles guiding the academy in its educational and enquiring mission. The pace and intensity of change over the past two decades or so, and the increasingly complex link to policy, societal, epistemic, ethical and technological developments, may, however, necessitate more thoughtful and purposive forms of questioning about the nature of the academy's engagement with the world.

In a context in which the pace of change is such that it shatters previous beliefs, habits of body and mind, and moral and intellectual moorings, I suggest that a significant role for the academy is to question, and to enable dialogic encounters to kindle the debate on how it relates to the world and can contribute to the shaping of a common future for humanity. The nature of this endeavour might bear on at least two fundamental and related areas of reflection that can provide openings beyond the immediate horizon. The first is ontological in nature and concerns the academy's relation to society and to the present and future shape of the world. The second is epistemological in nature and concerns the kind of knowledge that academics believe should be called upon to shore up this ontological questioning, and promote the empowerment of students as owners of a common future.

The opening up to society and societal issues is an underlying pattern in the history of the university since mediaeval times. At a time when inequalities both within and outside the academy are acutely visible and tangible, and increasingly difficult to legitimize as our understanding of the world improves, the issue of the relation of the academy to wider society is central. In an approach germane to Delanty's (2002: 46), who suggests that the role of the university is to provide structures for public debate 'to enable society to live with choice in a global world of uncertainty', and to Barnett's (2004: 252), for whom it must provide a space to enable individuals to 'prosper amid supercomplexity', my vision implies a significant public intellectual role for the academy and conveys a view of universities as dialogic democratic spaces engaging experts and non-experts. It relies for its accomplishment on the purposeful generation of modes of enquiry that provide means of dealing with instability, uncertainty, ambiguity, immediate replicability and vertiginous obsolescence whilst proposing ways of envisaging the future for what has materially become a common world.

This brings forth issues about the enactment of this vision in practice. Whether academics are resisting the neoliberal agenda or whether they are absorbed by it is not clear-cut. As accounts of practices reported in this book show, the environment in which academics work is rich, and allows for a multiplicity of enactments in which complex, competing and overlapping ideologies strive. The relation to the neoliberal agenda itself is complex and ambiguous. In order to avoid pondering unproductively over a 'past–future' dichotomy (the past was good; the future is bleak), the notion that new things and new knowledge emerge from existing things and existing knowledge is useful. Change theory tells us that turbulence is a natural condition for the emergence of something new, as ideas and practices are tested and contested in this turbulence and in the process adapted, adopted, shared or discarded.

It is therefore opportune to capitalize on the present tensions in the academy to strengthen engagement with differences while providing space to problematize them. In this vision, the academy sustains its historic purpose to be open, questioning and reflective but with a greater sense of interconnectivity and interdependency, and a heightened ability, translated into the curriculum, to deal with uncertainty and complexity. As a major shaper of the global future, the academy is a safe dialogic site for intellectual critique and global collaborations. It is engaged in developing strategies for facilitating ways of teaching and researching in universities that contribute to conceptualizing the world as common to all, shared by all, and sustainable only through preserving its plurality.

References

Abbas, A. and McLean, M. (2003) Communicative Competence and the Improvement of University Teaching: Insights from the Field. *British Journal of Sociology of Education* 24 (1): 69–81.

Al-Atiqi, I.M. and Alharbi, L.M. (2009) Meeting the Challenge: Quality Systems in Private Higher Education in Kuwait. *Quality in Higher Education* 15 (1): 5–16.

Allen, M. and Ainley, P. (2007) *Education Make You Fick, Innit?: What's Gone Wrong with England's Schools, Colleges and Universities and How to Start Putting It Right.* London: Tufnell Press.

Altbach, P.G. (2007) Peripheries and Centres: Research Universities in Developing Countries. *Higher Education Management and Policy* 19 (2): 111–134.

Altbach, P.G. and Knight, J. (2007) The Internationalization of Higher Education: Motivations and Realities. *Journal of Studies in International Education* 11 (3/4): 290–305.

Altbach, P.G. and McGill Peterson, P. (2008) Higher Education and the Global Marketplace. In D. Barker and A.W. Wiseman (eds) *The Worldwide Transformation of Higher Education, International Perspectives on Education and Society.* Bingley: Emerald JAI: 313–335.

Alvesson, M. (2002) *Understanding Organizational Culture.* London: Sage.

Alvesson, M. and Willmott, H. (2002) Identity Regulation as Organizational Control: Producing the Appropriate Individual. *Journal of Management Studies* 39 (5): 619–644.

Andreotti, V. (2006) Soft versus Critical Global Citizenship Education. *Policy and Practice: A Development Education Review* 3: 40–51. Available online: http://www.developmenteducationreview.com/issue3 (last accessed 11 February 2011).

Andreotti, V. (2008) Development vs. Poverty: Notions of Cultural Supremacy in Development Education Policy. In D. Bourn (ed.) *Development Education: Debates and Dialogues.* London: Institute of Education, University of London: 45–63.

Appadurai, A. (2000) Grassroots Globalization and the Research Imagination. *Public Culture* 12 (1): 1–19.

Appadurai, A. (2005) *Modernity at Large: Cultural Dimensions of Globalization.* Minneapolis: University of Minnesota Press. Revised edition.

Appiah, A. (2005) *The Ethics of Identity.* Princeton NJ: Princeton University Press.

Apple, M.W. (1993) *Official Knowledge: Democratic Education in a Conservative Age.* New York: Routledge.

Apple, M.W. (1995) *Education and Power*. New York: Routledge. 2nd edition.

Apple, M.W., Kenway, J. and Singh, M. (eds) (2005) *Globalizing Education: Policies, Pedagogies and Politics*. New York: Peter Lang.

Archer, M.S. (1995) *Realist Social Theory: The Morphogenetic Approach*. Cambridge: Cambridge University Press.

Archer, M.S. (2000) *Being Human: The Problem of Agency*. Cambridge: Cambridge University Press.

Arendt, H. (1958) *The Human Condition*. Chicago: University of Chicago Press.

Ashwin, P. (2009) *Analysing Teaching–Learning Interactions in Higher Education: Accounting for Structure and Agency*. London: Continuum.

Bailey, F.C. (1977) *Morality and Expediency: The Folklore of Academic Politics*. Oxford: Blackwell.

Ball, J.S. (ed.) (1994) *What Is Policy? Texts, Trajectories and Toolboxes*. London: Open University Press.

Ball, S.J. (2000) Performativities and Fabrication in the Education Economy: Towards the Performative Society? *Australian Educational Researcher* 27 (2): 1–24.

Ball, S.J. (2003) The Teacher's Soul and the Terrors of Performativity. *Journal of Education Policy* 18 (2): 215–228.

Ballantyne, R., Bain, J. and Packer, J. (1997) *Reflecting on University Teaching: Academics' Stories*. Canberra: Australian Government Publishing Service.

Barnett, R. (1994) *The Limits of Competence: Knowledge, Higher Education and Society*. Buckingham: Society for Research into Higher Education and Open University Press.

Barnett, R. (1997) *Higher Education: A Critical Business*. Buckingham: Society for Research into Higher Education and Open University Press.

Barnett, R. (2000) *Realising the University in an Age of Supercomplexity*. Buckingham: Society for Research into Higher Education and Open University Press.

Barnett, R. (2004) Learning for an Unknown Future. *Higher Education Research and Development* 23 (3): 247–260.

Barnett, R. (2005) *Reshaping the University: New Relationships between Research, Scholarship and Teaching*. Maidenhead: Society for Research into Higher Education and Open University Press.

Barnett, R. (2007) *A Will to Learn: Being a Student in an Age of Uncertainty*. Maidenhead: Society for Research into Higher Education and the Open University Press.

Barnett, R. (2011) *Being a University*. New York: Routledge.

Barnett, R. and Coate, K. (2005) *Engaging the Curriculum in Higher Education*. Maidenhead: Society for Research into Higher Education and Open University Press.

Barnett, R. and Di Napoli, R. (2008) *Changing Identities in Higher Education: Voicing Perspectives*. London: Routledge.

Baxter Magolda, M.B. (2009) Educating for Self-Authorship: Learning Partnerships to Achieve Complex Outcomes. In C. Kreber (ed.) *The University and its Disciplines: Teaching and Learning within and beyond Disciplinary Boundaries*. Oxford: Routledge: 143–156.

Becher, T. (1989) *Academic Tribes and Territories: Intellectual Enquiry and the Cultures of Disciplines*. Buckingham: Society for Research into Higher Education and Open University Press.

Becher, T. and Trowler, P. (2001) *Academic Tribes and Territories: Intellectual Enquiry and the Cultures of Disciplines*. Buckingham: Society for Research into Higher Education and Open University Press. 2nd edition.

Beck, U. (2006) *The Cosmopolitan Vision*. Cambridge: Polity Press.

Becker, J. (1993) *Human Capital: A Theoretical and Empirical Analysis, with Special Reference to Education*. Chicago: University of Chicago Press. 3rd edition.

Bernstein, B. (1997) Class and Pedagogies: Visible and Invisible. In A.H. Halsey, H. Lauder, P. Brown and A. Stuart Wells (eds) *Education: Culture, Economy, and Society*. Oxford: Oxford University Press: 59–79.

Bernstein, B. (2000) *Pedagogy, Symbolic Control and Identity: Theory, Research, Critique*. New York: Rowman and Littlefield. 2nd edition.

Berry, M. (2009) Les mirages de la bibliométrie, ou comment scléroser la recherche en croyant bien faire. *Revue du Mouvement Anti-utilitaire dans les Sciences Sociales: L'Université en crise: Mort ou résurrection?* 33: 166–183.

Bidan, M. and Dherment, I. (2009) Les pôles de compétitivité comme leviers cognitifs de création de valeur. *Revue Management et Avenir* 25 (5): 5–25.

Biggs, J. (1987) *Student Approaches to Learning and Study*. Melbourne: Australian Council for Educational Research.

Biggs, J. (2007) *Teaching for Quality Learning at University: What the Student Does*. Maidenhead: Society for Research into Higher Education and Open University Press. 3rd edition.

Biglan, A. (1973) The Characteristics of Subject Matter in Different Scientific Areas. *Journal of Applied Psychology* 57 (3): 195–203.

BIS (2009) *Higher Ambitions: The Future of Universities in a Knowledge Economy*. London: Department for Business, Innovation and Skills.

Blackwell, R. and McLean, M. (1996) Mentoring New University Teachers. *International Journal for Academic Development* 1 (2): 80–85.

Blackwell, R. and Blackmore, P. (2003) *Towards Strategic Staff Development in Higher Education*, Maidenhead: Society for Research into Higher Education and Open University Press.

Bleiklie, I. (1998) Justifying the Evaluative State: New Public Management Ideals in Higher Education. *European Journal of Education* 33 (3): 299–316.

Boffo, S. and Moscati, R. (1998) Evaluation in the Italian Higher Education System: Many Tribes, Many Territories . . . Many Godfathers. *European Journal of Education* 33 (3): 349–360.

Bourdieu, P. (1990) *Homo Academicus*. Translated by Peter Collier. Cambridge: Polity Press.

Bourdieu, P. and Passeron, J.-C. (1977) *Reproduction in Education, Society and Culture*. Translated by Richard Nice. London: Sage.

Bourn, D. (2008) *Development Education: Debates and Dialogues*. London: Bedford Way Papers.

Bourn, D. (2009) Students as Global Citizens. In E. Jones (ed.) *Internationalisation: The Student Voice*. London: Routledge.

Bourn, D., McKenzie, A. and Shiel, C. (2006) *The Global University: The Role of the Curriculum*. London: Development Education Association.

Boyer, E. (1990) *Scholarship Reconsidered: Priorities of the Professoriate*. Princeton, NJ: Carnegie Foundation for the Advancement of Teaching.

Boyer Commission (1998) Reinventing Undergraduate Education: A Blueprint for America's Research Universities. Available online: http://naples.cc.sunysb.edu/ Pres/boyer.nsf/ (last accessed 10 January 2011).

Brecher, J., Costello, T. and Smith, B. (2000) *Globalisation from Below: The Power of Solidarity*. Cambridge, MA: South End Press.

Brennan, J. (2007) The Academic Profession and Increasing Expectations of Relevance. In M. Kogan and U. Teichler (eds) *Key Challenges to the Academic Profession*. Paris and Kassel: International Centre for Higher Education Research Kassel: 19–28.

Brennan, J. and Shah, T. (2000) *Managing Quality in Higher Education*. Buckingham: Open University Press.

Brew, A. (2009) Academic Research in Contemporary Society. In M. Tight (ed.) *The Routledge International Handbook of Higher Education*. New York: Routledge: 473–485.

Brew, A. and Boud, D. (2009) Understanding Academics Engagement with Research. In A. Brew and L. Lucas (eds) *Academic Research and Researchers*. Maidenhead: Society for Research into Higher Education and the Open University Press: 189–203.

Brew, A. and Lucas, L. (eds) (2009) *Academic Research and Researchers*. Maidenhead: Society for Research into Higher Education and Open University Press.

Brockbank, A. and McGill, I. (2000) *Facilitating Reflective Learning in Higher Education*. Buckingham: Society for Research into Higher Education and Open University Press.

Brookfield, S. (1995) *Becoming a Critically Reflective Teacher*. San Francisco: Jossey Bass.

Brown, R. (2004) *Quality Assurance in Higher Education: The UK Experience since 1992*. London: RoutledgeFalmer.

Brown, R. (ed.) (2010) *Higher Education and the Market*. London: Routledge.

Brown, S. and Race, P. (2002) *Lecturing: A Practical Guide*. London: Kogan Page.

Buchanan, J., Gordon, S. and Schuck, S. (2008) From Mentoring to Monitoring: The Impact of Changing Work Environments on Academics in Australian Universities. *Journal of Further and Higher Education* 32 (3): 241–250.

Callon, M., Lascoumes, P. and Barthe, Y. (2001) *Acting in an Uncertain World: An Essay on Technical Democracy*. Cambridge, MA: MIT Press.

Carroll, M., Razvi, S., Goodliffe, T. and Al-Habsi, F. (2009) Progress in Developing a National Quality Management System for Higher Education in Oman. *Quality in Higher Education* 15 (1): 17–27.

Castells, M. (2010) *The Rise of the Network Society*. Malden, MA: Wiley-Blackwell. 2nd edition.

Chamayou, G. (2009) Petits conseils aux enseignants-chercheurs qui voudront réussir leur évaluation. *Revue du Mouvement Anti-utilitaire dans les Sciences Sociales: L'Université en crise: Mort ou résurrection?* 33: 146–165.

Clark, B.R. (1987) *The Academic Life: Small Worlds, Different Worlds*. Princeton: Carnegie Foundation for the Advancement of Teaching.

Clegg, S. (1999) Professional Education, Reflective Practice and Feminism. *International Journal of Inclusive Education* 3: 167–179.

Clegg, S. (2006) The Problem of Agency in Feminism: A Critical Realist Approach. *Gender and Education* 18 (3): 309–324.

Clegg, S. (2007) The Demotic Turn: Excellence by Fiat. In A. Skelton (ed.) *International Perspectives on Teaching Excellence in Higher Education: Improving Knowledge and Practice*. Abingdon: Routledge: 91–102.

Clegg, S. (2008) Academic Identities under Threat? *British Educational Research Journal* 34 (3): 329–345.

Clegg, S. and Smith, K. (2010) Learning, Teaching and Assessment Strategies in Higher Education: Contradictions of Genre and Desiring. *Research Papers in Higher Education* 25 (1): 115–132.

Cousin, G. (2008) Reconsidering Scholarship Reconsidered. In R. Murray (ed.) *The Scholarship of Teaching and Learning in Higher Education*. Maidenhead: Society for Research into Higher Education and Open University Press: 91–97.

Cousin, G. (2009) *Researching Learning in Higher Education: An Introduction to Contemporary Methods and Approaches*. New York: Routledge.

Cox, M.D. (1997) Long-Term Patterns in a Mentoring Program for Junior Faculty: Recommendations for Practice. *To Improve the Academy* 16: 225–268.

Cryer, P. (1981) Who Are the Staff Developers in UK Universities and Polytechnics? *Higher Education* 10 (4): 425–436.

D'Andrea, V.M. (ed.) (2009) Quality Developments in the Gulf. *Quality in Higher Education*, Special Issue 15 (1).

D'Andrea, V.M. and Gosling, D. (2005) *Improving Teaching and Learning in Higher Education: A Whole Institution Approach*. Maidenhead: Society for Research in Higher Education and Open University Press.

Darandari, E.Z., Al-Qahtani, S.A., Allen, I.D., Al-Yafi, W.A., Al-Sudairy, A.A. and Catapang, J. (2009) The Quality Assurance System for Post-Secondary Education in Saudi-Arabia: A Comprehensive, Developmental and Unified Approach. *Quality in Higher Education* 15 (1): 39–50.

Darder, A. (2002) *Reinventing Paulo Freire: A Pedagogy of Love*. Boulder, CO: Westview.

Darder, A. (2003) *After Race: Racism after Multiculturalism*. New York: New York University Press.

Davies, B., Gottsche, M. and Bansel, P. (2006) The Rise and Fall of the Neo-liberal University. *European Journal of Education* 41 (2): 305–319.

Dearlove, J. (1997) The Academic Labour Process: From Collegiality and Professionalism to Managerialism and Proletarianisation? *Higher Education Review* 30 (1): 56–75.

Deem, R. (2003) Managing to Exclude? Manager-Academic and Staff Communities in Contemporary UK Universities. In M. Tight (ed.) *International Perspectives on Higher Education Research: Access and Inclusion*. Amsterdam: Elsevier Science JAL: 103–125.

Deem, R., Hillyard, S. and Reed, M. (2007) *Knowledge, Higher Education, and the New Managerialism*. Oxford: Oxford University Press.

Delanty, G. (2001) *Challenging Knowledge: The University in the Knowledge Society*. Buckingham: Society for Research into Higher Education and Open University Press.

Delanty, G. (2002) The University and Modernity: A History of the Present. In K. Robins and F. Webster (eds) *The Virtual University?: Knowledge, Markets and Management*. New York: Oxford University Press: 31–48.

Delanty, G. (2008) Academic Identities and Institutional Change. In R. Barnett and R. Di Napoli (eds) *Changing Identities in Higher Education: Voicing Perspectives*. Abingdon: Routledge: 124–133.

Descombes, V. (2009) L'identité collective d'un corps enseignant. *Revue du Mouvement Anti-utilitaire dans les Sciences Sociales: L'Université en crise: Mort ou résurrection?* 33: 225–284.

Donald, J.G. (1995) Disciplinary Differences in Knowledge Validation. In N. Hativa and M. Marincovich (eds) *Disciplinary Differences in Teaching and Learning: Implications for Practice.* San Francisco: Jossey-Bass: 7–17.

Donald, J.G. (2002) *Learning to Think: Disciplinary Perspectives.* San Francisco: Jossey-Bass.

Donald, J. (2006) Enhancing the Quality of Teaching in Canada. In C. Kreber (ed.) *International Policy Perspectives on Improving Learning with Limited Resources.* San Francisco: Jossey Bass: 23–31.

Donald, J.G. (2009) The Commons: Disciplinary and Interdisciplinary Encounters. In C. Kreber (ed.) *The University and Its Disciplines: Teaching and Learning within and beyond Disciplinary Boundaries.* London: Routledge: 35–49.

Donnelly, J.F. (1999) Schooling Heidegger: On Being in Teaching. *Teaching and Teacher Education* 15: 933–949.

Dweck, C.S. (1999) *Self-Theories: Their Role in Motivation, Personality, and Development.* Philadelphia: Psychology Press.

Ecclestone, K. (1996) The Reflective Practitioner: Mantra or a Model for Emancipation. *Studies in the Education of Adults* 28 (2): 146–161.

Edmunds, R. and Richardson, J.T.E (2009) Conceptions of Learning, Approaches to Studying and Personal Development in UK Higher Education. *British Journal of Educational Psychology* 79 (2): 295–309.

Ellis, R., Goodyear, P., Brillant, M. and Prosser, M. (2008) Student Experiences of Problem-Based Learning in Pharmacy: Conceptions of Learning, Approaches to Learning, and the Integration of Face-to-Face and On-Line Activities. *Advances in Health Sciences Education* 13 (5): 675–692.

Engeström, Y. (2001) Expansive Learning at Work: Towards an Activity Theoretical Reconceptualization. *Journal of Education and Work* 14 (1): 133–156.

Engeström, Y., Miettinen, R. and Punamäki, R.-L. (eds) (1999) *Perspectives on Activity Theory.* Cambridge: Cambridge University Press.

Eraut, M. (2000) Non-Formal Learning, Implicit Learning and Tacit Knowledge in Professional Work. In F. Coffield (ed.) *The Necessity for Informal Learning.* Bristol: Policy Press: 12–31.

Etzkowitz, H. (2008) *The Triple Helix: University–Industry–Government Innovation in Action.* London: Routledge.

Evans, L. (2009) Location, Location, Location, and Acquiring the Ideal Home: A New Conception of Academic Practice. Paper presented at the annual conference of the Society for Research into Higher Education, 10 December, Celtic Manor Resort, Newport.

Falk, R. (1994) The Making of Global Citizenship. In B. van Steenbergenn (ed.) *The Condition of Citizenship.* London: Sage: 127–140.

Fanghanel, J. (2004) Capturing Dissonance in University Teacher Education Environments. *Studies in Higher Education* 29 (5): 575–590.

Fanghanel, J. (2007a) Local Responses to Institutional Change: A Discursive Approach to Positioning. *Studies in Higher Education* 32 (2): 187–205.

Fanghanel, J. (2007b) Teaching Excellence in Context: Drawing from a Socio-cultural Approach. In A. Skelton (ed.) *International Perspectives on Teaching Excellence in Higher Education.* Abingdon: Routledge: 197–212.

Fanghanel, J. (2007c) The Relation of Higher Education to the Economy: A Critical Role for the Research and Teaching Nexus? Available online: http://portal-live. solent.ac.uk/university/rtconference/colloquium_papers.aspx (last accessed 8 October 2010).

Fanghanel, J. (2009a) *Pedagogical Constructs: Socio-cultural Conceptions of Teaching and Learning in Higher Education*. Saarbrücken: VDM Verlag.

Fanghanel, J. (2009b) Exploring Teaching and Learning Regimes in Higher Education Settings. In C. Kreber (ed.) *The University and Its Disciplines: Teaching and Learning within and beyond Disciplinary Boundaries*. London: Routledge: 196–208.

Fanghanel, J. (2009c) The Role of Ideology in Academics' Conceptions of their Discipline. *Teaching in Higher Education*, Special Issue: Purposes, Knowledge and Identities 14 (5): 565–577.

Fanghanel, J. and Trowler, P. (2008) Exploring Academic Identities and Practices in a Competitive Enhancement Context: A UK-Based Case Study. *European Journal of Education* 43 (3): 301–313.

Fanghanel, J. and Cousin, G. (2012) 'Worldly' Pedagogy: A Way of Conceptualizing Teaching towards Global Citizenship. *Teaching in Higher Education* 17(1) (forthcoming).

Fenwick, T. (2003) Flexibility and Individualisation in Adult Education Careers: The Case of Portfolio Workers. *Journal of Education and Work* 16 (2): 165–184.

Finkelstein, M. (2007) The 'New' Look of Academic Careers in the United States. In M. Kogan and U. Teichler (eds) *Key Challenges to the Academic Profession*. Paris and Kassel: International Centre for Higher Education Research Kassel: 145–158.

Freire, P. (1996) *Pedagogy of the Oppressed*. London: Penguin.

Furedi, F. (2005) For Accreditation, See Indoctrination. *Times Higher Education Supplement*. Available online: http://www.timeshighereducation.co.uk/story.asp?se ctioncode=26&storycode=195891 (last accessed 2 February 2011).

Galaz-Fontes, J.F., Padilla-González, L. and Gil-Antón, M. (2007) The Increasing Expectation of Relevance for Higher Education and the Academic Profession: Some Reflections on the Case of Mexico. In M. Kogan and U. Teichler (eds) *Key Challenges to the Academic Profession*. Paris and Kassel: International Centre for Higher Education Research Kassel: 49–62.

Gappa, J.M., Austin, A.E. and Trice, A.G. (2007) *Rethinking Faculty Work: Higher Education's Strategic Imperative*. San Francisco: Jossey Bass.

Gibbons, M., Limoges, C., Nowotny, H., Schwartzman, S., Scott, P. and Trow, M. (1994) *The New Production of Knowledge: The Dynamics of Science and Research in Contemporary Societies*. London: Sage.

Gibbs, G. and Coffey, M. (2004) The Impact of Training of University Teachers on Their Teaching Skills, Their Approach to Teaching and the Approach to Learning of Their Students. *Active Learning in Higher Education* 5 (1): 87–100.

Giddens, A. (1984) *The Constitution of Society: Outline of the Theory of Structuration*. Cambridge: Polity Press.

Giddens, A. (1990) *The Consequences of Modernity*. Cambridge: Polity Press.

Goffman, E. (1959) *The Presentation of Self in Everyday Life*. New York: Doubleday Anchor Books.

Gordon, G. and Whitchurch, C. (2007) Managing Human Resources in Higher Education: The Implications of a Diversifying Workforce. *Higher Education Management and Policy* 19 (2): 135–155.

Gosling, D. and Hannan, A. (2007) Centres for Excellence in Teaching and Learning in England: Recognising, Celebrating and Promoting Excellence? In A. Skelton (ed.) *International Perspectives on Teaching Excellence in Higher Education*. Abingdon: Routledge: 147–166.

Griffiths, R. (2004) Knowledge Production and the Research–Teaching Nexus: The Case of the Built Environment Disciplines. *Studies in Higher Education* 29 (6): 709–726.

Guile, D. and Young, M.F.D. (2003) Transfer and Transition in Vocational Education: Some Theoretical Considerations. In T. Tuomi-Gröhn and Y. Engeström (eds) *Between School and Work: New Perspectives on Transfer and Boundary-Crossing*. Amsterdam: Pergamon: 63–81.

Halsey, A.H. (1982) The Decline of Donnish Dominion? *Oxford Review of Education* 8 (3): 215–229.

Halsey, A.H. and Trow, M.A. (1971) *The British Academics*. London: Faber and Faber.

Hannan, A. and Silver, H. (2000) *Innovating in Higher Education: Teaching, Learning and Institutional Cultures*. Buckingham: Society for Research into Higher Education and Open University Press.

Harland, T. (2009) The University, Neoliberal Reform and the Liberal Educational Ideal. In M. Tight, K.O. Mok, J. Huisman and C. Morphew (eds) *The Routledge International Handbook of Higher Education*. New York: Routledge: 511–521.

Hartwig, L. (2010) Diversification and Competition in the German Higher Education System. In R. Brown (ed.) *Higher Education and the Market*. New York: Routledge: 110–122.

Healey, M. (2000) Developing the Scholarship of Teaching in Higher Education: A Discipline-Based Approach. *Higher Education Research and Development* 19 (2): 169–189.

Healey, M. and Jenkins, M. (2009) *Developing Undergraduate Research and Inquiry*. York: Higher Education Academy.

Henkel, M. (2000) *Academic Identities and Policy Change in Higher Education*. London: Jessica Kingsley.

Henkel, M. (2005) Academic Identity and Autonomy in a Changing Policy Environment. *Higher Education* 49 (1/2): 155–176.

Hill, J. (2000) *On Becoming a Cosmopolitan: What It Means to Be a Human Being in the New Millennium*. Maryland: Roman and Littlefield.

Hounsell, D. and Anderson, C. (2009) Ways of Thinking and Practicing in Biology and History: Disciplinary Aspects of Teaching and Learning Environments. In C. Kreber (ed.), *The University and Its Disciplines: Teaching and Learning within and beyond Disciplinary Boundaries*. London: Routledge: 71–83.

Howe, N. and Strauss, W. (2000) *Millennials Rising: The Next Great Generation*. New York: Vintage Books.

Huber, M.T. (2004) *Balancing Acts: The Scholarship of Teaching and Learning in Academic Careers*. Washington, DC: Carnegie Foundation for the Advancement of Teaching and the American Association for Higher Education.

Huber, M.T. and Morreale, S.P. (eds) (2002) *Disciplinary Styles in the Scholarship of Teaching and Learning: Exploring Common Ground*. Washington, DC: American Association for Higher Education.

Huisman, J. (ed.) (2009) *International Perspectives on the Governance of Higher Education: Alternative Frameworks for Coordination*. New York: Routledge.

Hutchings, P. (2007) Theory: The Elephant in the Scholarship of Teaching and Learning Room. *International Journal for the Scholarship of Teaching and Learning* 1 (1). Available online: http://academics.georgiasouthern.edu/ijsotl/2007_v1n1.htm (last accessed 2 February 2011).

Hutchings, P. and Shulman, L.S. (1999) The Scholarship of Teaching: New Elaborations, New Developments. *Change* 31 (5): 10–15.

Hutchings, P. and Huber, M. (2008) Placing Theory in the Scholarship of Teaching and Learning. *Arts and Humanities in Higher Education* 7 (3): 229–244.

Jayaram, N. and Altbach, P.G. (2006) Confucius and the Guru: The Changing Status of the Academic Profession in China and India. *Journal of Educational Planning and Administration* 20 (4): 395–410.

Jones, A. (2009) Generic Attributes as Espoused Theory: The Importance of Context. *Higher Education* 58: 175–191.

Kaghed, N. and Kezaye, A. (2009) Quality Assurance Strategies of Higher Education in Iraq and Kurdistan: A Case Study. *Quality in Higher Education* 15 (1): 71–78.

Kandlbinder, P. and Peseta, T. (2009) Key Concepts in Postgraduate Certificates in Higher Education Teaching and Learning in Australasia and the United Kingdom. *International Journal of Academic Development* 14 (1): 19–31.

Kerr, C. (1963) *The Uses of the University*. Cambridge, MA: Harvard University Press.

King, R. (2004) *The University in a Global Age*. Basingstoke: Palgrave Macmillan.

Kinman, G., Jones, F. and Kinman, R. (2006) The Well-Being of the UK Academy, 1998–2004. *Quality in Higher Education* 12 (1): 15–27.

Knight, P. (2002) *Being a Teacher in Higher Education*. Buckingham: Society for Research into Higher Education and Open University Press.

Knight, P. (2006) *The Effects of Post-graduate Certificates: A Report to the Project Sponsor and Partners*. Milton Keynes: Open University Press. Available online: http://kn.open.ac.uk/public/document.cfm?docid=8640 (last accessed 12 February 2011).

Knight, P. and Saunders, M. (1999) Understanding Teachers' Professional Cultures through Interview: A Constructivist Approach. *Evaluation and Research in Education* 13 (3): 144–156.

Knight, P. and Trowler, P. (1999) It Takes a Village to Raise a Child: Mentoring and the Socialisation of New Entrants to the Academic Professions. *Journal of Mentoring and Tutoring* 7 (1): 23–34.

Kreber, C. (2005) Charting a Critical Course on the Scholarship of University Teaching Movement. *Studies in Higher Education* 30 (4): 389–405.

Kreber, C. (ed.) (2009) *The University and Its Disciplines: Teaching and Learning within and beyond Disciplinary Boundaries*. New York: Routledge.

Kuhn, T.S. (1970) *The Structure of Scientific Revolutions*. Chicago: University of Chicago Press. 2nd edition.

Kwiek, M. (2006) Emergent European Educational Policies under Scrutiny: The Bologna Process from a Central European Perspective. In V. Tomusk (ed.) *Creating the European Area of Higher Education: Voices from the Periphery*. Dordrecht: Springer: 87–115.

Lambert, C., Parker, A. and Neary, M. (2007) Entrepreneurialism and Critical Pedagogy: Reinventing the Higher Education Curriculum. *Teaching in Higher Education* 12 (4): 525–553.

Latour, B. (2009) Universitaires, encore un effort pour être autonomes. *Le Monde*, 25 February. Available online: http://www.bruno-latour.fr/presse/presse_art/31-UNIVERSITES.html (last accessed 2 February 2011).

Latour, B. (2010) *Cogitamus: Six Lettres sur les Humanités Scientifiques*. Paris: La Découverte.

Lave, J. and Wenger, E. (1999) Learning and Pedagogy in Communities of Practice. In J. Leach and B. Moon (eds) *Learners and Pedagogy*. London: Sage: 21–33.

Lindblom-Ylänne, S., Trigwell, K., Nevgi, A. and Ashwin, P. (2006) How Approaches to Teaching are Affected by Discipline and Teaching Context. *Studies in Higher Education* 31 (3): 285–298.

Lingard, B. and Ozga, J. (eds) (2007) *The RoutledgeFalmer Reader in Education Policy and Politics*. Abingdon: Routledge.

Lipsky, M. (1980) *Street Level Bureaucracy: Dilemmas of the Individual in Public Services*. Beverley Hills: Sage.

Locke, W. and Bennion, A. (2010a) *Supplementary Report to the HEFCE Higher Education Workforce Framework Based on the International Changing Academic Profession (CAP) Study*. London: Centre for Higher Education Research and Information (CHERI). Available online: http://www.open.ac.uk/cheri/pages/CHERI-Reports-2010.shtml (last accessed 1 February 2011).

Locke, W. and Bennion, A. (2010b) *The Changing Academic Profession: The UK and Beyond*. UUK Research Report. London: Centre for Higher Education Research and Information (CHERI). Available online: http://www.open.ac.uk/cheri/pages/CHERI-Reports-2010.shtml (last accessed 1 February 2011).

Longo, G. (2009) La bibliométrie et les gardiens de l'orthodoxie. *Revue du Mouvement Anti-utilitaire dans les Sciences Sociales: L'Université en crise: Mort ou résurrection?* 33: 141–145.

Lucas, L. (2004) Reclaiming Academic Research Work from Regulation and Relegation. In M. Walker and J. Nixon (eds) *Reclaiming Universities from a Runaway World*. Maidenhead: Open University Press: 35–50.

Lucas, L. (2006) *The Research Game in Academic Life*. Maidenhead: Society for Research into Higher Education and Open University Press.

Luke, A. (2007) After the Marketplace: Evidence, Social Science and Educational Research. In B. Lingard and J. Ozga (eds) *The RoutledgeFalmer Reader in Education Policy and Politics*. Abingdon: Routledge: 85–100.

Luke, C. (2000) One Step Up, Two Down: Women in Higher Education Management in South East Asia. In M. Tight (ed.) *Academic Work and Life: What Is It to Be an Academic and How This Is Changing*. New York: Elsevier Science: 285–305.

Lyotard, J.F. (1984) *The Postmodern Condition*. Translated by Geoff Bennington and Brian Massumi. Manchester: Manchester University Press.

McCulloch, A. (2009) The Student as Co-producer: Learning from Public Administration about the Student–University Relationship. *Studies in Higher Education* 34 (2): 171–183.

McCune, V. (2004) Development of First-Year Students' Conceptions of Essay Writing. *Higher Education* 47 (3): 257–282.

McCune, V. and Hounsell, D. (2005) The Development of Students' Ways of Thinking and Practising in Three Final-Year Biology Courses. *Higher Education* 49: 255–289.

Macfarlane, B. (2004) *Teaching with Integrity: The Ethics of Higher Education Practice*. London: RoutledgeFalmer.

Macfarlane, B. (2007) Beyond Performance in Teaching Excellence. In A. Skelton (ed.) *International Perspectives on Teaching Excellence in Higher Education: Improving Knowledge and Practice*. Abingdon: Routledge: 48–59.

Macfarlane, B. (2009) *Researching with Integrity: The Ethics of Academic Enquiry*. New York: Routledge.

Macfarlane, B. (2011) The Morphing of Academic Practice: Unbundling and the Rise of the Para-academic. *Higher Education Quarterly* 65 (1): 59–73.

Macfarlane, B. and Gourlay, L. (2009) The Reflection Game: Enacting the Penitent Self. *Teaching in Higher Education* 14 (4): 455–459.

Malcolm, J. and Zukas, M. (2009) Making a Mess of Academic Work: Experience, Purpose, and Identity. *Teaching in Higher Education* 14 (5): 495–506.

Manathunga, C. (2006) Doing Educational Development Ambivalently: Applying Post-colonial Metaphors to Educational Development? *International Journal for Academic Development* 11 (1): 19–29.

Mann, S. (2001) Alternative Perspectives on the Student Experience: Alienation and Engagement. *Studies in Higher Education* 26 (1): 7–19.

Marginson, S. (2007) National and Global Competition in Higher Education. In B. Lingard, and J. Ozga (eds) *The RoutledgeFalmer Reader in Education Policy and Politics*. London: Routledge: 131–153.

Marginson, S. (2008) Global Field and Global Imagining: Bourdieu and Worldwide Higher Education. *British Journal of Sociology of Education* 29 (3): 303–315.

Martin, E. (1999) *Changing Academic Work: Developing the Learning University*. Buckingham: Society for Research into Higher Education and Open University Press.

Martin, R. and Sunley, P. (2003) Deconstructing Clusters: Chaotic Concept or Policy Panacea. *Journal of Economic Geography* 3: 5–35.

Marton, F. and Säljö, R. (1976) On Qualitative Differences in Learning II: Outcome as a Function of the Learner's Conception of the Task. *British Journal of Educational Psychology* 46: 115–127.

Marton, F., DallAlba, G. and Beaty, E. (1993) Conceptions of Learning. *International Journal of Educational Research* 19 (3): 277–300.

Meek, L.V. (2007) Internationalisation of Higher Education and the Australian Academic Profession. In M. Kogan and U. Teichler (eds) *Key Challenges to the Academic Profession*. Paris and Kassel: International Centre for Higher Education Research Kassel: 65–80.

Merton, R.K. (1968) *Social Theory and Social Structure*. New York: New York Free Press.

Moon, J. (2004) *A Handbook of Reflective and Experiential Learning: Theory and Practice*. London: RoutledgeFalmer.

Muller, J. (2009) Forms of Knowledge and Curriculum Coherence. *Journal of Education and Work* 22 (3): 205–226.

Musselin, C. (2007) Transformation of Academic Work: Facts and Analysis. In M. Kogan and U. Teichler (eds) *Key Challenges to the Academic Profession*. Paris and Kassel: UNESCO Forum for Higher Education, Research and Knowledge: 175–190.

Musselin, C. (2009) Les réformes des universités en Europe: Des orientations comparables, mais des déclinaisons nationales. *Revue du Mouvement anti-utilitariste dans les sciences sociales: L'Université en crise. Mort ou résurrection?* 33: 69–91.

Naidoo, R. (2005) Universities in the Marketplace: The Distortion of Teaching and Research. In R. Barnett (ed.) *Reshaping the University: New Relationships between Research, Scholarship and Teaching*. Maidenhead: Society for Research into Higher Education and Open University Press: 27–47.

Naidoo, R. and Jamieson, I. (2005) *Knowledge in the Marketplace: The Global Commodification of Teaching and Learning in Higher Education*. Dordrecht: Springer.

NCIHE (1997) *Higher Education in the Learning Society*. Report of the National Committee of Inquiry into Higher Education. London: HMSO.

Neary, M. and Winn, J. (2009) The Student as Producer: Reinventing the Student Experience in Higher Education. In M. Neary, H. Stevenson and L. Bell (eds) *The Future of Higher Education: Pedagogy, Policy and the Student Experience*. London: Continuum: 126–138.

Neave, G. (1998) The Evaluative State Reconsidered. *European Journal of Education* 33 (3): 265–283.

Neumann, R. (2001) Disciplinary Differences and University Teaching. *Studies in Higher Education* 26 (2): 135–146.

Neumann, R., Parry, S. and Becher, T. (2002) Teaching and Learning in Their Disciplinary Contexts: A Conceptual Analysis. *Studies in Higher Education* 27 (4): 405–417.

Newman, J.H. (1852) The Idea of a University. Available online: http://www.newmanreader.org/works/idea/ (last accessed 12 February 2011).

Newton, J. (2000) Feeding the Beast or Improving Quality? *Quality in Higher Education* 6 (2): 153–163.

Nixon, J. (2004) Learning the Language of Deliberative Democracy. In M. Walker and J. Nixon (eds) *Reclaiming Universities from a Runaway World*. Buckingham: Society for Research into Higher Education and Open University Press: 114–127.

Nixon, J. (2011) *Higher Education and the Public Good: Imagining the University*. London: Continuum International.

Nussbaum, M.C. (2000) *Women and Human Development: The Capabilities Approach*. Cambridge: Cambridge University Press.

Nussbaum, M.C. (2003) Women's Education: A Global Challenge. *Signs* 29 (2): 325–355.

Ozga, J. (2000) *Policy Research in Educational Settings: Contested Terrain*. Buckingham: Open University Press.

Ozga, J., Dahler-Larsen, P., Segerholm, C. and Simola, H. (eds) (2011) *Fabricating Quality in Education: Data and Governance in Europe*. Abingdon: Routledge.

Paradeise, C. and Lichtenberger, Y. (2009) Universités: réapprendre la responsabilité collégiale. *Revue du Mouvement Anti-utilitaire dans les Sciences Sociales : L'Université en crise: Mort ou résurrection?* 33: 226–243.

Parker, S. (1997) *Reflective Teaching in the Postmodern World: A Manifesto for Education in Postmodernity*. Buckingham: Open University Press.

Perry, W.G. (1970) *Forms of Intellectual and Ethical Development in the College Years: A Scheme*. New York: Holt, Rinehart and Winston.

Phillips, A. (2007) *Multiculturalism without Culture*. Princeton, NJ: Princeton University Press.

Prichard, C. (2000) *Making Managers in Universities and Colleges*. Buckingham: Society for Research into Higher Education and Open University Press.

Prosser, M. and Trigwell, K. (1999) *Understanding Learning and Teaching: The Experience in Higher Education*. Buckingham: Society for Research into Higher Education and Open University Press.

Prosser, M., Rickinson, M., Bence, V., Hanbury, A. and Kulej, M. (2006) Formative Evaluation of Accredited Programmes. Available online: http://search3.openobjects.com/kb5/hea/evidencenet/resource.page?record=Z5dlbhV4oyw   (last accessed 3 January 2011).

Ramsden, P., Batchelor, D., Peacock, A., Temple, P. and Watson, D. (2010) *Enhancing and Developing the National Student Survey: Report to HEFCE*. London: Institute of Education. Available online: http://www.hefce.ac.uk/pubs/rdreports/2010/rd12_10/ (last accessed 22 January 2011).

Ravinet, P. (2008) From Voluntary Participation to Monitored Coordination: Why European Countries Feel Increasingly Bound by Their Commitment to the Bologna Process. *European Journal of Education* 43 (3): 353–367.

Readings, B. (1996) *The University in Ruins*. Cambridge, MA: Harvard University Press.

Reay, D., David, M. and Ball, S.J. (2001) Making a Difference?: Institutional Habituses and Higher Education Choice. Available online: http://www.socresonline.org.uk/5/4/reay.html (last accessed 10 February 2011).

Rhoades, G. (1998) *Managed Professionals: Unionized Faculty and Restructuring Academic Labour*. Albany, NY: State University of New York Press.

Rice, R.E. (2006) Enhancing the Quality of Teaching and Learning: The US Experience. In C. Kreber (ed.) *International Policy Perspectives on Improving Learning with Limited Resources*. San Francisco: Jossey-Bass: 13–22.

Rizvi, F. (2007) Debating Globalization and Education after September 11. In B. Lingard, and J. Ozga (eds) *The RoutledgeFalmer Reader in Education Policy and Politics*. London: Routledge: 23–35.

Robeyn, I. (2006) Three Models of Education: Rights, Capabilities and Human Capital. *Theory and Research in Education* 4: 69–84.

Robins, K. and Webster, F (eds) (2002) *The Virtual University?: Knowledge, Markets, and Management*. Oxford: Oxford University Press.

Rowland, S. (2008) Collegiality and Intellectual Love. *British Journal of Sociology of Education* 29 (3): 353–360.

Roxå, T. and Mårtensson, K. (2008) Strategic Educational Development: A National Swedish Initiative to Support Change in Higher Education. *Higher Education Research and Development* 27 (2): 155–168.

Roxå, T. and Mårtensson, K. (2009) Teaching and Learning Regimes from Within: Significant Networks as a Locus for the Social Construction of Teaching and Learning. In C. Kreber (ed.) *The University and Its Disciplines: Teaching and Learning within and beyond Disciplinary Boundaries*. London: Routledge: 209–218.

Roxå, T., Olsson, T. and Mårtensson, K. (2008) Appropriate Use of Theory in the Scholarship of Teaching and Learning as a Strategy for Institutional Development. *Arts and Humanities in Higher Education* 7: 276–294.

Salter, B. and Tapper, T. (1994) *The State and Higher Education*. Ilford: Woburn Press.

Santiago, R. and Carvalho, T. (2008) Academics in a New Work Environment: The Impact of New Public Management on Work Conditions. *Higher Education Quarterly* 62 (3): 204–223.

Saunders, M. and Warburton, T. (1997) Teachers Subject Cultures: Accommodating the National Curriculum in Maths and Technology. In G. Helsby and G. McMulloch (eds) *Teachers and the National Curriculum*. London: Cassell: 78–95.

Saunders, M. and Machell, J. (2000) Understanding Emerging Trends in Higher Education Curricula and Work Connections. *Higher Education Policy* 13: 287–302.

Sawyer, R. (2002) Unresolved Tensions in Sociocultural Theory: Analogies with Contemporary Sociological Debates. *Culture and Psychology* 8 (3): 283–305.

Schön, D.A. (1983) *The Reflective Practitioner*. San Francisco: Jossey-Bass.

Schultz, T. (1963) *The Economic Value of Education*. New York: Columbia University Press.

Scott, I. (2003) Balancing Excellence, Equity and Enterprise in a Less-Industrialised Country: The Case of South Africa. In G. Williams (ed.) *The Enterprising University: Reform, Excellence and Equity*. Buckingham: Society for Research into Higher Education and Open University Press: 40–53.

Scott, P. (1995) *The Meanings of Mass Higher Education*. Buckingham: Society for Research into Higher Education and the Open University Press.

Scott, P. (2009) Foreword. In A. Brew and L. Lucas (eds) *Academic Research and Researchers*. Maidenhead: Society for Research into Higher Education and Open University Press: xiii–xviii.

Sen, A. (1985) *Commodities and Capabilities*. Amsterdam: New Holland.

Sen, A. (1999) *Development as Freedom*. New York: Knopf.

Sen, A. (2002) *Rationality and Freedom*. Cambridge, MA: Belknap Press.

Senge, P.M. (1990) *The Fifth Discipline: The Art and Practice of the Learning Organization*. London: Century Business.

Shuell, T.J. (1986) Cognitive Conceptions of Learning. *Review of Educational Research* 56 (4): 411–436.

Shulman, L.S. (2005) Signature Pedagogies in the Professions. *Daedalus* 134 (3): 52–59.

Singh, M. (2005) Responsive Education: Enabling Transformative Engagements with Transitions in Global/National Imperatives. In M.W. Apple, J. Kenway and M. Singh (eds) *Globalizing Education: Policies, Pedagogies and Politics*. New York: Peter Lang Publishing: 113–134.

Skelton, A. (2005) *Understanding Teaching Excellence in Higher Education: Towards a Critical Approach*. Abingdon: Routledge.

Skelton, A. (2007) *International Perspectives on Teaching Excellence in Higher Education: Improving Knowledge and Practice*. Abingdon: Routledge.

Slaughter, L. and Rhoades, G. (2004) *Academic Capitalism and the New Economy: Markets, State, and Higher Education*. Baltimore: Johns Hopkins University Press.

Slaughter, S. and Leslie, L. (1997) *Academic Capitalism: Politics, Policies, and the Entrepreneurial University*. Baltimore: John Hopkins University Press.

Smith, K. (2008) Who Do You Think You're Talking To? The Discourse of Learning and Teaching Strategies. *Higher Education* 56: 395–406.

Streeting, W. and Wise, G. (2009) Rethinking the Values of Higher Education: Consumption, Partnership, Community? Available online: http://www.qaa.ac.uk/students/studentengagement/undergraduate.pdf (last accessed 15 January 2011).

Tapper, T. (2007) *The Governance of British Higher Education: The Struggle for Policy Control*. Dordrecht: Springer.

Taylor, P. (1999) *Making Sense of Academic Life: Academics, Universities and Change*. Buckingham: Society for Research into Higher Education and Open University Press.

Taylor, P. (2008) Being an Academic Today. In R. Barnett and R. Di Napoli (eds) *Changing Identities in Higher Education*. Abingdon: Routledge: 27–39.

Taylor, P. and Wilding, D. (2009) Rethinking the Values of Higher Education: The Student as Collaborator and Producer? Undergraduate Research as a Case Study. Available online: http://www.qaa.ac.uk/students/studentEngagement/Undergraduate.pdf (last accessed 15 January 2010).

Thomas, R. and Davies, A. (2005) Theorizing the Micro-politics of Resistance: New Public Management and Managerial Identities in the UK Public Services. *Organization Studies* 26: 683–706.

Tierney, W. (1987) The Semiotic Aspects of Leadership: An Ethnographic Perspective. *American Journal of Semiotics* 5: 233–250.

Tight, M. (2003) *Researching Higher Education*. Maidenhead: Society for Research into Higher Education and Open University Press.

Tomusk, V. (2003) The War of Institutions, Episode 1: The Rise, and the Rise of Private Higher Education in Eastern Europe. *Higher Education Policy* 16: 213–238.

Tomusk, V. (ed.) (2006) *Creating the European Area of Higher Education: Voices from the Periphery*. Dordrecht: Springer.

Trigwell, K. and Ashwin, P. (2006) An Exploratory Study of Situated Conceptions of Learning and Learning Environments. *Higher Education* 51: 243–258.

Trow, M. (1973) *Problems in the Transition from Elite to Mass Higher Education*. Berkeley, CA: Carnegie Commission on Higher Education.

Trow, M. (1994) Managerialism and the Academic Profession: The Case of England. *Higher Education Policy* 7 (2): 11–18.

Trow, M. (2002) Some Consequences of the New Information and Communication Technologies for Higher Education. In K. Robins and F. Webster (eds) *The Virtual University?: Knowledge, Markets, and Management*. Oxford: Oxford University Press: 301–317.

Trowler, P. (1998) *Academics Responding to Change: New Higher Education Frameworks and Academic Cultures*. Buckingham: Society for Research into Higher Education and Open University Press.

Trowler, P. (2008) *Culture and Change in Higher Education: Theories and Practices*: Palgrave Macmillan.

Trowler, P., Fanghanel, J. and Wareham, T. (2005) Freeing the Chi of Change: The Higher Education Academy and Enhancing Teaching and Learning in Higher Education. *Studies in Higher Education* 30 (4): 427–444.

Tuomi-Gröhn, T. and Engeström, Y. (eds) (2003) *Between School and Work: New Perspectives on Transfer and Boundary-Crossing*. Oxford: Pergamon.

Unterhalter, E. (2003) The Capabilities Approach and Gendered Education: An Examination of South African Complexities. *Theory and Research in Education* 1 (1): 7–22.

Unterhalter, E. (2005) Global Inequality, Capabilities, Social Justice and the Millennium Development Goal for Gender Equality in Education. *International Journal of Educational Development* 25 (2): 111–122.

Urry, J. (2002) Globalizing the Academy. In K. Robins and F. Webster (eds) *The Virtual University?: Knowledge, Markets, and Management*. Oxford: Oxford University Press: 20–30.

Van Manen, M. (1991) Reflectivity and the Pedagogical Moment: The Normativity of Pedagogical Thinking and Acting. *Curriculum Studies* 23 (6): 507–536.

Vatin, F. and Vernet, A. (2009) La crise de l'Université française: une perspective historique et socio-démographique. *Revue du Mouvement Anti-utilitaire dans les Sciences Sociales: L'Université en crise: Mort ou résurrection?* 33: 47–68.

Walker, M. (2006) *Higher Education Pedagogies: A Capabilities Approach*. Maidenhead: Society for Research into Higher Education and Open University Press.

Walker, M. and Nixon, J. (eds) (2004) *Reclaiming Universities from a Runaway World*. Maidenhead: Open University Press.

Welch, A. (2005) Challenge and Change: The Academic Profession in Uncertain Times. In A. Welch (ed.) *The Professoriate: Profile of a Profession*. Dordrecht: Springer: 1–19.

Wenger, E., McDermott, R. and Snyder, W. (2002) *A Guide to Managing Knowledge: Cultivating Communities of Practice*. Boston, MA: Harvard Business School Press.

Wheelahan, L. (2007) How Competency-Based Training Locks the Working Class out of Powerful Knowledge: A Modified Bernsteinian Analysis. *British Journal of Sociology of Education* 28 (5): 637–651.

Wheelahan, L. (2009) The Problem with CBT (and Why Constructivism Makes Things Worse). *Journal of Education and Work* 22 (3): 227–242.

Whitchurch, C. (2008a) Beyond Administration and Management. In R. Barnett and R. Di Napoli (eds) *Changing Identities in Higher Education*. Abingdon: Routledge: 67–88.

Whitchurch, C. (2008b) Shifting Identities and Blurring Boundaries: The Emergence of Third Space Professionals in UK Higher Education. *Higher Education Quarterly* 62 (4): 377–396.

White, N.R. (2007) The Customer Is Always Right?: Student Discourse about Higher Education in Australia. *Higher Education* 54: 593–607.

Winter, R. (2009) Academic Manager or Managed Academic? Academic Identity Schisms in Higher Education. *Journal of Higher Education Policy and Management* 31 (2): 121–131.

Yang, Y.-F. and Tsai, C.-C. (2010) Conceptions of and Approaches to Learning through Online Peer Assessment. *Learning and Instruction* 20 (1): 72–83.

Yosso, T. (2005) Whose Culture Has Capital? A Critical Race Theory Discussion of Community Cultural Wealth. *Race Ethnicity and Education* 8 (1): 69–91.

Young, M.F.D. (1971) *Knowledge and Control: New Directions for the Sociology of Education*. London: Collier-Macmillan.

Young, M.F.D. (2008) *Bringing Knowledge Back In: From Social Constructivism to Social Realism in the Sociology of Education*. Abingdon: Routledge.

Young, M. (2009) What Are Schools For? In H. Daniels, H. Lauder and J. Porter (eds) *Knowledge, Values and Educational Policy: A Critical Perspective*. London: Routledge: 10–18.

Index

Abbas, A. and McLean, M. 29
academic endeavour 1, 2, 16,
115; compromise of 106, 117;
endorsement of change and
complexity in 119; future of 99,
119; inherent features of 119;
mercantilism and 104–5, 113;
performativity and 113; practice of,
ideological positioning and 9; senior
ranks, 'restrictions on access' to 22–3;
social understanding of, deficiency
in 4; utilitarian aims and 87; values,
centrality of 85
academic experiences: academic values,
international scholarship and clashes
of 105; access to higher education,
broadening of 79; alienation of
students, fighting against 64;
authentic engagement 108; co-
learning and collaboration 60–1;
complexity, help in understanding
112; complexity in teaching
and learning 70; conception of
discipline, complexity in 77–8;
creative process, aim of facilitation
of 76; creative process, facilitation
of 45; critical literacy, Andreotti
on 62–3; cultural difference,
prejudices about 59; cultural flow,
direction in global narrative 102–3;
deficiency conceptions 57–8; desire
and challenge 63–4; disciplinary
contexts, knowledge and evidence
differences between 42; disciplinary
idiosyncrasies 71; documentation
23; emerging economies, academics
in 106–7; ethical dilemmas, human
rights issues and 106; expertise,

reality gap and 40–1; facilitative
teaching, normalization of views
on 59; frustration and anxiety in
teaching 64; generic skills, promotion
of 76; hard work and effort, part
of student journey 60; ideological
dissonance 45–6; ideological drive
78–9; informal learning in practice
39–40; intensification of work
22; international scholarship 103,
104–5; junior academics, powers
of 44; language ability, attitudes
to 105–6; learning as commodity
56–7; learning outcomes, realism on
64; local inequalities, globalization
and exacerbation of 107; long-
standing practices, prevalence
of 44; mentoring 60; mutual
relationship of learners and teachers
24; National Student Survey (NSS,
UK) 55; participation and diversity,
problem of notions of 58; PGCerts
34–5; plurality, Arendt on 109;
preparation time 23; promotion
structures, research performance and
90–1; qualifications as currency 57;
research and teaching, competing
institutional agendas on 90; risk-
aversion 26; seminar-like teaching
64; streamlining of practice 25–6;
student as becoming 59; student as
consumer 57; student as deficient
57, 58; student as recipient of
desire to teach 63–4; student as
vehicle for social transformation 57,
61–3; students' views on worldly
pedagogies 111, 112; teacher-centred
approaches 75; teaching to learning

outcomes 56; technology, role of 75; unreflective compliance 23–4; western responsibility, globalization and issue of 107; work demands 22; work-related skills, importance of 79; world order, higher education and change in 78–9; writing and learning 43; *see also* vignettes
academic freedom 9–10
academic presence 100–3
academic values, educational ideologies and 7–10
academics: academic trajectory, Boyer's conception of academic role 4–5; academic values and educational ideologies 7–10; beliefs and values 2; conformity, ritualism and identity 6; crisis of professoriate for 5–6; disciplinary commitment and dissemination of generic knowledge, dichotomy between 2; disciplines of, conceptions of 72–4, 80–1; economic imperatives and work of 5; educational ideologies and 2, 7–10; espoused conceptions 1; experience of research, engagement with 89–91; identity 6; individuality and identity 6; labour of, lack of social understanding of 4; lived practice of, ideological positioning and 9; multi-faceted complexity of roles 2; professional and intellectual engagement 1, 4–6; reflexive actions 29–30; roles 1–2; ubiquitousness of work of 2, 23, 100; value tensions inherent in positioning of 7; variation between groups, 'portfolio careers' and 5
access: to abstract knowledge 39; to agents 10; to context-independent knowledge 8; to 'deliberative democracy' 112; democratization of 3; equity of access to globalized academe 107–8; to foreignness, globalization and 103; inequality of 79–80, 100, 113, 117; to meta-cognition skills 56; to 'powerful knowledge' 8, 46, 111; to research, institutional agendas and 90; to senior ranks, restrictions on 22–3; social order and access to resources 7
accountability, self-regulation and 17

agency: access to agents 10; collective 11; purposefulness in 10–11; reality and 11; structure and 10–11
Al-Atiqui, I.M. and Alharbi, L.M. 19
alienation: notion of 49; of students, fighting against 64
Allen, M. and Ainley, P. 62
Altbach, P.G. 86
Altbach, P.G. and Knight, J. 104
Altbach, P.G. and McGill Peterson, P. 104
alternatives to LtT programmes 37–8, 46–7
Alvesson, M. 71
Alvesson, M. and Willmott, H. 11
Andreotti, V. 62–3, 98, 109
Appadurai, A. 85, 89, 94, 100
Appiah, A. 108, 112
Apple, M.W. 9, 62, 109
Apple, M.W., Kenway, J. and Singh, M. 62, 100
application, disciplinary focus on 76–8
Archer, M.S. 10, 11
Arendt, H. 97, 108–9, 112
Ashwin, P. 11
Australia 9, 19, 31, 32, 34, 88, 91, 101, 102, 103–6, 115; Survey of Student Engagement (AUSSE) 53
authentic engagement 108
authenticity and identity 28–9, 29–30

Bailey, F.C. 4
Ball, S.J. 10, 20, 24, 26, 28, 29, 50
Ballantyne, R., Bain, J. and Parker, J. 66
Barnett, R. 9, 14, 35, 36, 55, 61, 85, 117, 118; academic globalism 97, 98, 108, 109, 112; learning to teach in higher education 35, 36
Barnett, R. and Coate, K. 55, 61, 109
Barnett, R. and Di Napoli, R. 3, 81, 85, 116
Baxter Magolda, M.B. 49
Becher, T. 4, 66, 67, 68, 69, 71–2, 86
Becher, T. and Trowler, P. 66, 71
Beck, U. 102, 106, 108, 110, 112
Becker, J. 7
becomingness conceptions 59–61, 65
beliefs and values 2
Bernstein, B. 9, 60
Berry, M. 88
Bidan, M. and Dherment, I. 88
Biggs, J. 25, 49, 56

Biglan, A. 68–9
Blackwell, R. and Blackmore, P. 35
Blackwell, R. and McLean, M. 37
Bleiklie, I. 9, 17, 18
Boffo, S. and Moscati, R. 9
Bologna 17, 19, 20
Bourdieu, P. 11, 84
Bourdieu, P. and Passeron, J.-C. 9, 10, 58
Bourn, D. 62, 109
Bourn, D., McKenzie, A. and Shiel, C. 109
Boyer, E. 4–5, 92
Boyer Commission Report (1998) 61
Brecher, J., Costello, T. and Smith, B. 100
Brennan, J. 27
Brennan, J. and Shah, T. 18–19
Brew, A. 94
Brew, A. and Boud, D. 91
Brew, A. and Lucas, L. 88
Brockbank, A. and McGill, I. 36
Brookfield, S. 36
Brown, R. 4, 5, 16, 17, 19, 24
Brown, S. and Race, P. 35
Buchanan, J., Gordon, S. and Schuck, S. 38

Callon, M., Lascoumes, P. and Barthe, Y. 85, 89, 96
Canada 19, 101
Carroll, M. *et al.* 19
Castells, M. 101
Chamayou, G. 88
change: causal theories of 35; change theory 119; endorsement of change and complexity 119; pace of 118; stability and, balance between 117–18
China 19–20
Clark, B.R. 69–70
Clegg, S. 6, 11, 27, 28–9, 36
Clegg, S. and Smith, K. 10, 20
co-learning and collaboration 60–1
collective agency 11
complexities of globalization 97–8, 102–3, 112–13
complexity: conception of discipline, complexity in 77–8; help in understanding 112; in teaching and learning 70
compromise of academic endeavour 106, 117

conformity, ritualism and identity 6
connectivity 100–3, 119
consumers or customers, students as 48, 56–7, 65
contestation of globalization 97
context, learning to teach (LtT programmes) and 31–4, 46
context-independent knowledge, access to 8
cosmopolitanism 99, 108, 109, 112
Cousin, G. 92, 94
Cox, M.D. 37
creative process: aim of facilitation of 76; facilitation of 45
crisis of professoriate 5–6
critical literacy, Andreotti on 62–3
Cryer, P. 32
cultural flows: direction in global narrative 102–3; globalization and 112–13
curriculum 25, 35, 37, 41, 42, 49, 62, 67, 80, 93, 116; belief and interpretation 50; curriculum 'alignment,' notion of 56; ideologies in, issue of 111; medical curriculum 68; ontological dimension of 61; production ideology 76, 77; properties of 55; values, place in 99; vision for 119

D'Andrea, V.M. 19
D'Andrea, V.M. and Gosling, D. 19, 31, 35
Darandari, E.Z. *et al.* 19
Darder, A. 62, 109
data, respondents and 12
Davies, B., Gottsche, M. and Bansel, P. 18, 23, 26
Dearlove, J. 4, 5
Deem, R. 20
Deem, R., Hillyard, S. and Reed, M. 3, 15, 16, 17, 18, 20, 23, 28, 88, 115
deficiency conceptions 57–9
Delanty, G. 63, 86, 99, 117, 118
'deliberative democracy,' access to 112
democratization: of access 3; potential of alternative modes of research 96
departments, relation of disciplines to 69–71
Descombes, V. 88
desire to teach, student as recipient of 63–4, 65

digital art and cultural history 75
disciplinary commitment and dissemination of generic knowledge, dichotomy between 2
disciplinary communities 66
disciplinary cultures 71–2
disciplinary idiosyncrasies 71
disciplines, engagement with 13, 66–81, 116; academics' conceptions of their disciplines 72–4, 80–1; application, focus on 76–8; departments, relation of disciplines to 69–71; disciplinary communities 66; disciplinary cultures 71–2; distinctions between 69; epistemological, focus on 74–6; epistemological entities, disciplines as 68–9; induction, focus on 74–6; institutions, relation of disciplines to 69–71; plurality of voices, emphasis on 81; production ideologies 76–8; reproduction ideologies 74–6; social critique, disciplines as 78–80; status of disciplines 66–8; transformation ideologies 78–80; work world, focus on preparation for 76–8
documentation 23
Donald, J.G. 19, 68, 69
Donnelly, J.F. 36
Dweck, C.S. 57

Ecclestone, K. 36
economic imperatives 3; and work of academics 5
Edmunds, R. and Richardson, J.T.E. 49
education: ideologies of 2, 7–10; as 'public good,' notion of 17
Ellis, R. et al. 49
empowerment (and potential for) 7, 14, 44, 46–7, 78, 99, 110–11, 113, 114–18; disempowerment 36
Engeström, Y. 41
Engeström, Y., Miettinen, R. and Punamäki, R.-L. 11
epistemological, disciplinary focus on 74–6
epistemological entities, disciplines as 68–9
epistemological factors 87
equity of access to globalized academe 107–8
Eraut, M. 36
espoused conceptions, academics and 1

ethical dilemmas, human rights issues and 106
Etzkowitz, H. 86
Europe 88, 104, 107; Central and Eastern 20, 83; managerialism and performativity from perspective of 20; networks in 104; Northern 9, 19, 31, 32; QA mechanisms in 19
European Union (EU) 102
Evans, L. 4
excellence, managerialism and 26–8
expertise, reality gap and 40–1

fabrication, generation of 29
facilitative teaching, normalization of views on 59
Falk, R. 100, 102
Fanghanel, J. 10, 11, 12, 20, 28, 57, 61; disciplines, engagement with 66, 67, 68, 71, 76; learning to teach in higher education 35, 43, 46
Fanghanel, J. and Cousin, G. 12, 110
Fanghanel, J. and Trowler, P. 12, 23
Fenwick, T. 5
financial burden, shift to students of 17
Finkelstein, M. 5
flaws in global flows 103–8, 112–13, 117
foreignness, globalization and access to 103
Foucault, M. 36
fragmentation of control 17
France 9
Freire, P. 9, 62, 109
funding: hybrid models of 17; of managed research 82
Furedi, F. 34–5
future of academic endeavour 99, 119

Galaz-Fontes, J.F., Padilla-González, L. and Gil-Antón, M. 5
Gappa, J.M., Austin, A.E. and Trice, A.G. 3, 5, 9
geography and geopolitics 106
Germany 9
Gibbons, M. et al. 3, 86
Gibbs, G. and Coffey, M. 39, 40
Giddens, A. 10, 11, 12, 29, 99, 100
global academic life 101–2
globalization 3, 14, 97–113, 117; academic presence 100–3; complexities of 97–8, 102–3, 112–

13; connectivity 100–3; contestation of subject 97; cultural flows 102–3, 112–13; flaws in global flows 103–8, 112–13, 117; global stakes for the academy 98–9, 112–13; networks and networked societies 100–3; theorization of 99–100; virtual academic globalism 102; worldliness, Arendt's concept of 97; worldly becoming 108–12, 113
Goffman, E. 4
Gordon, G. and Whitchurch, C. 5
Gosling, D. and Hannan, A. 27, 28
governance of higher education 16–18
Griffiths, R. 95
Guile, D. and Young, M.F.D. 42, 115
Gulf States 19

Halsey, A.H. 69–70
Halsey, A.H. and Trow, M.A. 66
Hannan, A. and Silver, H. 27
Harland, T. 4
Hartwig, L. 88
Healey, M. 95
Healey, M. and Jenkins, M. 60, 61, 94
Henkel, M. 6, 20, 66–7, 68, 69, 70
Higher Ambitions: The Future of Universities in a Knowledge Economy (Mandelson, P.) 50–1, 52
Hill, J. 108
Hounsell, D. and Anderson, C. 49, 68, 69
Howe, N. and Strauss, W. 55
Huber, M.T. 93, 95
Huber, M.T. and Morreale, S.P. 95
Huisman, J. 17
human capital approach 7
humanization in research 82–3, 96
Humboldt 7, 45; scholarship tradition of 4, 86
Hutchings, P. 93
Hutchings, P. and Huber, M. 93, 94
Hutchings, P. and Shulman, L.S. 95

identity 6; authenticity and 28–9, 29–30; individuality and 6; performativity cultures and 20–2; problematization of 63
ideology 3; academic values, educational ideologies and 7–10; dissonances in LtT programmes 44–6; intention and 8, 9; liberal ideologies 8;

underpinnings of LtT programmes 34–6; *see also* production ideologies; reproduction ideologies; transformation ideologies
induction, disciplinary focus on 74–6
inequalities: of access 79–80, 100, 113, 117; local inequalities, globalization and exacerbation of 107
informal learning in practice 39–40
information science, librarians and 77–8
innovation, managerialism and 26–8
institutions: institutional autonomy 9–10; relation of disciplines to 69–71
intellectual engagement 1, 4–6
intention, ideology and 8, 9
interconnectivity 98, 119
interdependency 10, 86, 98, 119
international scholarship 103, 104–5
intersubjectivity 11
interview data 12
invisible pedagogy 60

Jayaram, N. and Altbach, P.G. 20
Jones, A. 50

Kaghed, N. and Kezaye, A. 19
Kandlbinder, P. and Peseta, T. 32, 35
Kerr, C. 86
King, R. 3, 5, 86, 88, 99, 100, 117
Kinman, G., Jones, F. and Kinman, R. 22
Knight, P. 35, 37, 39–40, 44
Knight, P. and Saunders, M. 12
Knight, P. and Trowler, P. 37, 38
knowledge 3; abstract knowledge, access to 39; context-dependent knowledge 8, 56, 66, 67, 111; context independent knowledge 8; disciplinary contexts, knowledge and evidence differences between 42; experiential 9, 38, 56, 111–12; nature of 49, 67, 69, 86, 87; peer-reviewed 8, 39, 50; 'powerful knowledge,' access to 8, 46, 111; propositional knowledge 8, 111, 112, 117; reproduction ideologies and 8–9; situated knowledge 42; tacit knowledge 36; theories of 31, 110, 111, 113, 117; theory of 111, 113, 117; transfer knowledge 44
Kreber, C. 66, 95

Kuhn, T.S. 68
Kwiek, M. 20

Lambert, C., Parker, A. and Neary, M. 55, 61
language ability, attitudes to 105–6
Latour, B. 10, 85, 89
Lave, J. and Wenger, E. 11
learning: as commodity 56–7; as goal in itself approach 7; innovative approaches to teaching and 26–7; learning organizations 46–7; meaning of learning and teaching in higher education 50–1; mutual relationship of learners and teachers 24; outcomes of, realism on 64; to teach in higher education 32–4; writing and 43
learning to teach (LtT programmes) 13, 31–47, 115–16; alternatives to programmes 37–8, 46–7; context 31–4, 46; ideological dissonances 44–6; ideological underpinnings 34–6; impact of programmes 38–40; learning about teaching, sources for 37; learning organizations 46–7; professionalization, challenges of 46; reality gap 40–1; structural obstacles 43–4; theoretical underpinnings 34–6, 46; transfer, question of 41–3
liberal ideologies 8
Lindblom-Ylänne, S. *et al.* 69
Lingard, B. and Ozga, J. 3
Lipsky, M. 20
Locke, W. and Bennion, A. 5, 88
Longo, G. 88
Lucas, L. 86, 88, 91
Luke, A. 3, 23
Lyotard, J.F. 3, 18, 24, 115

McCulloch, A. 60–1
McCune, V. 49
McCune, V. and Hounsell, D. 49, 69
Macfarlane, B. 2, 5, 53, 85
Macfarlane, B. and Gourlay, L. 36
Malcolm, J. and Zukas, M. 2
managed academic, terminology of 15–16
managed research: issues in 88–9; *see also* research, engagement with
managerialism 3, 13, 15–30, 115; authenticity and identity 28–9, 29–30; deprofessionalization of academic work 16; excellence 26–8; fabrication, generation of 29; governance of higher education 16–18; identity, authenticity and 28–9, 29–30; identity, performativity cultures and 20–2; innovation 26–8; instantiations of 15–16; managed academic 15–16; management in operation 16; massification drift 16; neoliberal governance and 16; performativity and 18–20, 21–2, 23, 24–5, 26, 28–9; practice, performativity cultures and 20–2; 'remote steering,' governance by 16–17; streamlining of practice 25–6, 29; transparency of work 23–5; visualization of work 23–5, 29; work intensification 22–3, 29
Manathunga, C. 35
Mandelson, P. 50–1
Mann, S. 49, 64
Marginson, S. 17, 88, 100
market mechanisms 3, 17, 52
market theory 17
Martin, E. 28
Martin, R. and Sunley, P. 88
Marton, F. and Säljö, R. 49
Marton, F., DallAlba, G. and Beaty, F. 49
Meek, L.V. 5
mentoring 60
mercantilism 104–5, 113
Merton, R.K. 6
meta-cognition skills, access to 56
Moon, J. 36
Muller, J. 67
multiculturalism 63, 67, 99, 106, 110, 113, 117
multimodality 13, 85, 87, 116–17
Musselin, C. 3–4, 5–6, 9, 17, 18, 20, 88, 117

Naidoo, R. 88, 104
Naidoo, R. and Jamieson, I. 17
National Student Survey (NSS, UK) 48; conceptions of learning in 53–6
NCIHE (National Committee of Inquiry into Higher Education) 32
Neary, M. and Winn, J. 60, 94
Neave, G. 16–17
neo-conservative traditionalism 8
neo-universalism 98–9, 113

neocolonialism 99, 113
neoliberal agenda: impact on academic
    practices 117–18; resistance to or
    absorption by 118–19
neoliberal policies, academic roles and
    99
neoliberal trends in governance 17–18
networks and networked societies 100–3
Neumann, R. 68, 69
Neumann, R., Parry, S. and Becher, T. 68
New Zealand 31, 32, 34, 53, 115
Newman, Cardinal J.H. 7, 45, 86
Newton, J. 28
Nixon, J. 7, 16, 17, 98, 99, 108, 109,
    112
Nussbaum, M.C. 7, 59, 62, 94, 95

obsolescence 3, 98, 118
OECD (Organization for Economic
    Cooperation and Development) 3
Ozga, J. 3, 67
Ozga, J. et al. 19

Paradeise, C. and Lichtenberger, Y. 86
Parker, S. 36
participation and diversity, problem of
    notions of 58
pedagogical methodologies 62
performativity 36, 39, 55, 82, 88, 113,
    115; academic endeavour and 113;
    identity and performativity cultures
    20–2; managerialism and 18–20,
    21–2, 23, 24–5, 26, 28–9
Perry, W.G. 49
PGCerts 34–5
phenomenographic tradition 49
Phillips, A. 106
plurality: Arendt on 109; preservation of
    109, 117; promotion of 81, 99, 119;
    sustainability and 110, 112, 119; of
    voices, emphasis on 81
policy making and practice, contrasting
    discourses of 48, 49–52, 65
'portfolio careers' 5
post-constructivism 10
practice, moments of 13–14;
    performativity cultures and 20–2; see
    also disciplines, engagement with;
    globalization; learning to teach;
    managerialism; research, engagement
    with; students and learning,
    conceptions of

preparation time 23
Prichard, C. 20
production ideologies 7, 8, 114;
    disciplines, engagement with 76–8;
    students and learning, conceptions
    of 48
professional engagement 1, 4–6
professionalization, challenges of 46
promotion structures, research
    performance and 90–1
Prosser, M. and Trigwell, K. 49
Prosser, M. et al. 40
psychology-oriented perspectives 49
purposefulness in agency 10–11

qualifications as currency 57
Quality Assurance Agency (QAA, UK)
    19, 49
quality assurance (QA) 19
quality enhancement (QE) 19

Ramsden, P. et al. 53
Ravinet, P. 19
Readings, B. 3, 5
reality: agency and 11; reality gap in LtT
    programmes 40–1
Reay, D., David, M. and Ball, S.J. 9
reflexive actions 29–30
regulation, principles of 17
replicability 3, 98, 118
reproduction ideologies 7–8, 114–15;
    disciplines, engagement with 74–6;
    students and learning, conceptions
    of 48
research, engagement with 13–14, 82–
    96, 116–17; academics, experience
    of 89–91; democratizing potential
    of alternative modes 96; funding
    managed research 82; humanization
    82–3, 96; institutional agendas
    and access to research 90; issues in
    managed research 88–9; research
    modes, articulation of alternatives
    82–3, 91–5, 95–6; research space,
    pressures on 82; researcher's profile
    83–4; shaping of research field 86–7;
    socio-historical evolution of research
    space 86; trends in research space
    84–5
respondents, data and 12
Rhoades, G. 5, 15–16
Rice, R.F. 10

risk-aversion 26
Rizvi, F. 97
Robeyn, I. 7
Robins, K. and Webster, F. 3, 4, 100, 112
roles: fashioning of 29–30; neoliberal policies, academic roles and 99; practice and 1–2, 4, 6, 12–13; of socio-historical and epistemological factors 87; specificity in, endorsement of 27, 28
Rowland, S. 2
Roxå, T. and Mårtensson, K. 32, 71
Roxå, T., Olsson, T. and Mårtensson, K. 94
Russian Federation 20

Salter, B. and Tapper, T. 3
Santiago, R. and Carvalho, T. 5
Saunders, M. and Machell, J. 7
Saunders, M. and Warburton, T. 10, 20
Sawyer, R. 10
Schön, D.A. 36
Schultz, T. 7
Scott, P. 17, 19, 84–5, 89–90, 96, 117
self-actualization 29, 115
self-regulation, accountability and 17
Sen, A. 7
Senge, P.M. 46
Shuell, T.J. 49
Shulman, L.S. 68
Singh, M. 109
Skelton, A. 27, 28
Slaughter, L. and Rhoades, G. 5
Slaughter, S. and Leslie, L. 88
Smith, K. 10
social critiques, disciplines as 78–80
social order and access to resources 7
social practice theory 11
social transformation, students as vehicles for 61–3, 65
social world, concept of 10
socio-historical factors 87
sociological analysis of students and learning 48–9
South Africa 19, 101, 102, 103, 106, 107
status of disciplines 66–8
streamlining of practice 25–6, 29
Streeting, W. and Wise, G. 48
structural obstacles in LtT programmes 43–4

structuration theory 11
structure and agency 10–11
students and learning, conceptions of 13, 48–65, 116; alienation, notion of 49; becomingness conceptions 59–61, 65; consumers or customers, students as 48, 56–7, 65; deficiency conceptions 57–9; desire to teach, student as recipient of 63–4, 65; National Student Survey (NSS, UK), conceptions of learning in 53–6; phenomenographic tradition 49; policy making and practice, contrasting discourses of 48, 49–52, 65; production ideologies 48; psychology-oriented perspectives 49; reproduction ideologies 48; social transformation, students as vehicles for 61–3, 65; sociological analysis 48–9; student as becoming 59; student as consumer 57; student as deficient 57, 58; student as recipient of desire to teach 63–4; student as vehicle for social transformation 57, 61–3; students' views on worldly pedagogies 111, 112; transformation ideologies 48
supercomplexity 14, 61–2, 63, 97, 108, 117, 118

Tapper, T. 3, 5, 16, 17, 18, 91
Taylor, P. 20, 37, 68
Taylor, P. and Wilding, D. 49, 60, 61
technology 3, 5; role of 75
theoretical frameworks 7, 12, 87, 96
theoretical stance (of this book) 114–15
theoretical underpinnings of LtT programmes 34–6, 46
theories of knowledge 31, 110, 111, 113, 117
theories of the mind 68
theorization of globalization 99–100
Thomas, R. and Davies, A. 10
Tierney, W. 71
Tight, M. 92–3
Tomusk, V. 20
transfer, question in LtT programmes of 41–3
transformation ideologies 8, 9, 115; disciplines, engagement with 78–80; students and learning, conceptions of 48

transparency of work 23–5
trends in research space 84–5
Trigwell, K. and Ashwin, P. 49
Trow, M. 3, 16, 66
Trowler, P. 6, 7, 8, 11, 20, 29, 35, 67, 70, 72
Trowler, P., Fanghanel, J. and Wareham, T. 32, 35
Tuomi-Gröhn, T. 41
Tuomi-Gröhn, T. and Engeström, Y. 41–2, 115

ubiquitousness of work 2, 23, 100
uncertainty, complexity and 14, 63, 85, 98, 108, 114, 117, 118, 119
United States 9–10, 15, 16, 31, 37, 53, 69, 84, 101; Academic Quality Improvement Program 19; Higher Education Commission (HEC) 19; National Survey of Student Engagement (NSSE) 53
universities 2–3; change factors at work 3; diversity of 4; evolution of, constant nature of 3–4; history of, societal issues and 118; ideology and 3; management of quality in 18–19; organization of 3; politics and 3; safe sites for intellectual critique, role as 117
unreflective compliance 23–4
Unterhalter, E. 62
Urry, J. 100
utilitarian aims 87

values: centrality to academic endeavour of 85; international scholarship and clashes of 105; value tensions inherent in positioning of academics 7

Van Manen, M. 36
Vatin, F. and Vernet, A. 86
vignettes 12; global academic life 101–2; innovative approaches to teaching and learning 26–7; learning to teach in higher education 32–4; meaning of learning and teaching in higher education 50–1; performativity agenda 21–2; research, approach to 83–4; see also academic experiences
virtual academic globalism 102
visualization of work 23–5, 29

Walker, M. 7, 62, 109
Walker, M. and Nixon, J. 28, 62, 109
Weber, M. 35
Welch, A. 5, 66, 67
welfare state: decline of 3; questioning of 16
Wenger, E., McDermott, R. and Snyder, W. 11
Wheelahan, L. 67
Whitchurch, C. 2, 5
White, N.R. 48
Winter, R. 15–16
work: intensification of, managerialism and 22–3, 29; world of, disciplinary focus on preparation for 76–8
world order, higher education and change in 78–9
worldliness, Arendt's concept of 97
worldly becoming 108–12, 113
worldly pedagogy 110
writing and learning 43

Yang, Y.-F. and Tsai, C.-C. 49
Yosso, T. 9, 58, 62
Young, M.F.D. 7, 8–9, 41, 62, 67, 111